THE
ARTS
COUNCIL
OF ENGLAND

ACTING WITH INTENT:
theatre companies and their education programmes

Dick Downing
Mary Ashworth
Alison Stott

INVESTOR IN PEOPLE

Published in April 2002
by the National Foundation for Educational Research,
The Mere, Upton Park, Slough, Berkshire SL1 2DQ

CONTENTS

ACKNOWLEDGEMENTS

The authors wish to thank the following for their co-operation and contributions towards the report:

- the staff of the ten case study theatre companies who generously gave of their time to be interviewed

- the project steering group at the Arts Council of England – Ian Tabron (North West Arts Board), Jo Hemmant (London Arts Board), Norinne Betjamin and Isobel Hawson (ACE) and Martin McCallum (Drama Panel, ACE)

- John Harland, Director of NFER Northern Office, and Gail McIntyre, theatre director, who worked on the design of the research and gave advice throughout the process

- Hilary McEddery and Sue Medd for their secretarial support at NFER.

EXECUTIVE SUMMARY

The study

With the overall aim of encouraging good practice through the clarification of the aims and activities of theatre company education work, the research reported here addressed four key objectives:

♦ to analyse the aims and purposes of education work in theatre companies;

♦ to examine how these aims are translated into practice;

♦ to investigate the relationship between the educational work and the overall artistic mission of the theatre companies and how the identity of a theatre company relates to their education policy; and

♦ to use the results of the research to inform developments in the policy and practice of theatre company education activity and to develop the policy of funding bodies to better suit the needs of companies and artists.

The research adopted a case-study approach based on a purposive random sample of ten theatre companies. Initially, a random sample of 20 theatre companies was selected from an Arts Council list of theatre companies receiving Arts Council or Regional Arts Board funding in excess of £50,000. From this random sample, ten were chosen to reflect a range of different styles and types of theatre companies, and other criteria including type of funding category, main target groups and geographical spread. Quality of educational practice and provision was not considered as a criterion for selection. These ten companies were invited to participate in the research, and all agreed to take part. Interviews were conducted between May and September 2000.

Theatre companies' educational aims

The pattern of aims described by the interviewees was complex and diverse, and intentions were frequently interrelated.

Analysis of company members' responses produced five broad categories of aims, each with its own set of sub-categories. The five main categories are identified in Chapter 2 as follows:

♦ educational aims totally integrated with artistic aims;

♦ drama/theatre-centred educational aims;

- curriculum development and support aims;
- client-centred educational aims; and
- aims relating to the needs of theatre companies.

'Client-centred' aims (i.e. those relating to the personal development of individual participants and/or community development) emerged as an overriding preoccupation, with notably more citations than either curriculum-centred aims or those concerned with theatre companies' artistic or financial survival. Three companies claimed that educational aims were totally integrated with core artistic aims.

Three distinct but interrelated interpretations of the role of theatre in education were apparent in the data:

- a means of communication through emotion and/or the imagination which challenges preconceptions, and extends and enhances understanding of ourselves and others;
- a source of opportunities for self-expression which empowers individuals and generates self-esteem by allowing them to take risks, and release potential creativity; and
- a collective/community artform.

The majority of companies acknowledged changes in their educational aims over recent years. In some cases, companies had undertaken a radical reappraisal of their overall mission. In others, the development of opportunities for collaboration, with schools or through partnerships with other organisations, had accelerated their educational activities. Most also reported an increase in educational activity.

Within theatre companies, the support of the Chief Executive and the Board, and good internal communications, were seen as important factors in the management and delivery of education work.

In addition to long-term funding, many interviewees contended that greater flexibility in funding arrangements would enable them to be more creative, and more effective, in achieving their educational goals. Funding from various sources beyond their core or long-term funding had enabled all ten companies to develop their education work.

Translating aims into practice

Chapter 3 investigated the practice that emerges from the key aims. Using one project example from each company, it was possible to identify some recurrent features both in the generation and nature of education projects.

In the vast majority of cases, projects were originated and managed by core company staff, while being delivered or mediated by freelance staff. Many projects were the result of partnerships between arts organisations. The reliance on freelance staff, and the various implications of this way of working, have been a recurrent feature of the research.

The projects that were described divided fairly evenly between two broad types:

♦ those that supported, or were supported by, core artistic product; and

♦ participatory activities, using the theatre expertise available to the company, designed with particular sectors of the community in mind.

In some cases, the education project described was part of the core activity of the company.

The education projects described targeted a wide range of participants of various ages, from within and outside the formal education sector, including various community groupings. It became very clear from project descriptions that audience development and the delivery of education aims were frequently outcomes deriving from the same activity.

Projects that might deliver aims relating to curriculum development and teacher support were much less prevalent than those with 'client-centred' aims. Evaluation was approached enthusiastically by some, and cautiously by others. This in part reflected resource limitations, but in some cases revealed a scepticism about the impact of an investment in evaluation.

Education programmes and core artistic activity

Apart from financial, managerial and administrative integration, education work appeared to be integrated with the rest of a theatre's work in three different ways. For some companies, **education was the core activity**; for some, **education projects supported, or were supported by, the core artistic activity**; and for others, **education projects ran parallel to the core artistic activity**, and were not integrated. Several companies combined more than one form of integration. There was a general belief that resources were best used through integration, but this was qualified by the fear that one side – usually the core artistic imperative – might overwhelm the other.

It was widely agreed that the education work undertaken by companies was dependent on the maintenance of quality in the core artistic work they undertook, and that this was a fundamental resource for the education work. In its turn, the education work was generally seen to contribute to the well-being of the parent theatre company.

Overarching issues and themes

Defining education projects

Companies classified a very wide range of projects as 'educational', in particular blurring the distinction between education and community development.

The role of theatres in the formal education context

Of the ten theatres studied as part of this research, nine worked in or with schools, but to varying extents. Most of the education work they undertook in schools was the result of proactive initiatives by the theatre companies. This was often informed by dialogue with educators, and some companies maintained regular forums or channels of communication. However, even where such forums did exist or have existed, several companies indicated that there were difficulties in sustaining a productive dialogue.

There was recognition of the pressures teachers were under, and a perception that they experienced a lack of manoeuvrability in accommodating or exploiting the contribution of theatre companies, and that they suffered from a lack of time to plan with companies.

It may well be appropriate to encourage opportunities or channels for improving understanding and communication between the two sides, possibly regenerating what many believe to have been a stronger relationship between theatre companies and teachers, as individuals or collectively, in the past.

Continuity, development and progression

The high level of enthusiasm, sophistication and commitment in the companies studied could well produce even greater returns if certain factors were addressed. Questions were raised concerning a perceived trend towards more short-term project funding for education work, and away from more long-term, secure funding. One result of this was an apparent reliance on freelance staffing to undertake the education work, which possibly inhibited the development of both the education product and relationships with schools. Concern was also expressed that the pool of available and experienced freelance education workers was depleting.

The following approaches emerged as potentially valuable in addressing the concerns of theatre companies:

♦ a more accessible provision of training opportunities for those engaged in theatre education work;

♦ improved communication and dialogue between companies;

♦ some increase in the capacity to employ more education project mediators long term; and

♦ a more proactive approach to gathering the views of freelance workers.

1. THE STUDY

1.1 Background to the research

Since the early 1970s a considerable expansion has taken place in the provision of education programmes by regional theatres and touring companies. In part this has been inspired by the growing expectation that publicly funded arts organisations should provide education programmes as part of, or alongside, their core artistic activities. There has also been a substantial growth in the demand and opportunities for theatre education work, as the value of theatre has gained recognition in broader educational contexts.

The expansion which has taken place may have prompted many working within the theatre education sector to re-evaluate the essential aims and purposes of the work which they provide. Accordingly, questions are raised about the extent to which there is consensus between theatre professionals about the essential aims and purposes of the education work which they provide, and the agendas which it addresses.

In the formal education sector, while many new opportunities have become available, many more have been severely squeezed. LEA advisory structures have been largely dismantled, leaving large numbers of schools to take individual responsibility for developing arts subjects. However, in spite of financial and timetable difficulties, the appetite for external drama inputs seems to continue.

Many regional repertory theatres continue to face serious financial difficulties, and the position of education departments and activities can often seem vulnerable. The trend towards short-term project funding, especially for education projects, may have an impact on longer-term planning and the continuity and development of education programmes. Concerns over a lack of a secure career structure for theatre staff have also been voiced.

Collaborative working, and partnerships between organisations, have been one response to the need to make funds stretch as far as possible. Working to one agenda, using one budget, is not necessarily any longer the norm, and the resultant interconnections can create a fruitful, but sometimes confused situation.

All of these background factors were taken into account in the formation of the aims and objectives for the research, and are thus addressed within the report.

1.2   Aims of the research

With the overall aim of encouraging good practice through the clarification of the aims and activities of theatre company education work, the research addressed four key objectives:

♦   to analyse the aims and purposes of education work in theatre companies;

♦   to examine how these aims are translated into practice;

♦   to investigate the relationship between the educational work and the overall artistic mission of the theatre companies and how the identity of a theatre company relates to their education policy; and

♦   to use the results of the research to inform developments in the policy and practice of theatre company education activity and to provide information to develop the policy of funding bodies to better suit the needs of companies and artists.

It must be noted that this research, whilst examining the nature of theatre companies' education programmes, does not attempt to evaluate, assess or appraise those activities. The purpose of the sample is to understand the intentions behind a range of educational work – not to judge its quality or the outcomes for the participants.

1.3   Methods

The research adopted a case-study approach based on a purposive random sample of ten theatre companies. Initially, a random sample of 20 theatre companies was selected from an Arts Council list of theatre companies receiving Arts Council or Regional Arts Board funding in excess of £50,000. From this random sample, ten were chosen to reflect a range of different styles and types of theatre companies, and other criteria including type of funding category, main target groups and geographical spread. Quality of educational practice and provision was not considered as a criterion for selection. These ten companies were invited to participate in the research, and all agreed to take part. Interviews were conducted between May and September 2000.

Prior to the case study visits, a range of documentation was collected including artistic and education policies, a list of recent educational programmes, lists of core staff, Board members and advisory groups, and financial information and business plans.

Researchers then spent between one and three days visiting the individual theatre companies in the sample, and interviewing a range of personnel and freelance workers. A total of 63 interviews was completed – 43 in person and 20 on the telephone. Table 1.1 summarises the numbers of interviewees:

Table 1.1   Summary of interviewees

Interviewees	In person	By telephone
Board members	7	2
Chief executives, administrative directors, general managers	9	1
Artistic directors	8	2
Heads of education, education officers	6	–
Freelancers	3	12
Others: Including an assistant director, an associate director, two development and press officers, a tour and development officer, a marketing director, a community director, an arts coordinator, a director of a collaborating theatre company, a designer, a head of production, an administrator and a county drama adviser	10	3
Total	43	20

Source: *NFER, Theatre company and artists' education programmes*

The interviewees were offered confidentiality and anonymity, and hence, none of the theatre companies are named in the report.

1.4   Summary of theatre companies sample

This section introduces the ten theatre companies involved in the research – exploring their organisation, operating contexts and background and thus setting the scene for the chapters which follow. The companies were chosen to reflect the complete range of theatre provision.

1.4.1 Type of theatre company

Within the sample, a variety of theatre companies and provision were identified. Although numbers were divided equally between those that were closely associated with a theatre venue, and those whose main remit was to tour work to other venues, there was still considerable variation even within this classification.

Five of the companies comprised the traditional notion of a theatre company – located in, and highly dependent on, a specific theatre building. Four of these five were essentially regional repertory theatres – although one had an unusually large geographical and artistic remit, and one was a theatre 'in the round'. The other company was specifically defined as a 'children's theatre' – the building and performances clearly reflecting this. To greater or lesser extents, all of these theatres received touring work, and toured their own work to other venues.

The other five theatre companies were essentially touring companies that did not have buildings or accommodation which they described as theatre performance spaces. The touring companies varied to an even greater extent than the building-based theatres. One of the companies was established specifically to provide opportunities for black theatre artists, and another existed to produce work for a youth audience. Another addressed rural issues within the local community, and yet another brought together theatre companies from around the world into a festival of international theatre.

1.4.2 Theatre company size

There was a substantial, and immediately perceptible, difference in the sizes of the ten theatre companies involved in the research. However, precisely quantifying the sizes of the companies was difficult because of their differing operating structures, policies and activities. Theatre companies were also seen to be increasingly dependent on freelance workers – the numbers of which were constantly changing.

The largest company in the sample – a regional repertory company based in a significant theatre building complex – had 150 permanent staff, according to the head of education. Other building-based repertory companies varied between eight and 50 permanent staff.

The two smallest companies (both specialised touring companies) had only three permanent staff each – an artistic director, a general manager and an administrator. The other touring companies ranged from seven to 12 permanent staff. It is notable, and perhaps unsurprising, that in general, the largest theatre companies, in terms of permanent staff numbers, were those with established theatre buildings, and the companies with the fewest permanent members of staff were the touring companies.

1.4.3 Organisational structure and management

Surprisingly, despite other variations between the theatre companies in the sample, remarkably similar organisational structures were apparent. The hierarchical structure invariably consisted of a Board of Directors at the top, a chief executive (often artistic and administrative directors) then individual functions or departments.

All of the theatre companies in the sample relied on a Board of directors or a Board of management at the head of the organisation. The Boards were made up of between seven and 15 individuals, and two theatre company Boards had three and four observers respectively. The role and responsibilities of Boards varied from those with a purely overseeing role, to individual Board members who offered practical advice and assistance in the running of the theatre.

For nine out of the ten companies in the sample, the role of chief executive was assumed by one or more of: the artistic director, administrative director, general manager or producer – reporting directly to the Board of management. In the remaining theatre, the largest in the sample, there was a separate chief executive role which formed an additional link between the artistic/administrative directors and the Board. For practical purposes, the main day-to-day management of all of the theatres was conducted by the chief executive, artistic or administrative directors and a senior management team made up of the heads of individual departments. However, in the smaller of the theatre companies, these roles tended to blur considerably, with all of the permanent members of staff being heavily involved in many of the different management activities.

Thinking specifically about education, it is clear that the different theatre companies had very different ways of addressing their educational aims and priorities, and an equally different array of ways of providing and managing education functions within their organisational structure. Some of the theatre companies chose to have dedicated education staff, or an education department, and some chose to split the education functions across a number of different personnel. In some cases, particularly those companies producing work for children or young people, education pervaded the organisations so completely that it was difficult to identify roles which were not, in some way, related to their education function.

Chapter 4 includes additional discussion of the status of education within the different companies, and the role of the education officer in determining that status.

1.4.4 Social contexts

It is clear than in addition to their different sizes and venues, the theatre companies in the sample also addressed widely differing social contexts.

For the touring companies, social contexts resulted from the general social issues of the time – although some also addressed local and regional issues relating to their location. For example, the touring company specialising in productions for young people in youth clubs often addressed issues of key importance for those young people, such as drug abuse or teenage pregnancy, although they also dealt with issues of local importance. Similarly, the social context of the theatre festival came primarily from its work with international artists, although it was becoming increasingly attached to its local community.

For the building-based theatre companies, social context was far more clearly determined by their location, and the relationship with their local and regional community. One regional repertory theatre relied heavily on the support of the local community, as a small theatre in close proximity to several cities with larger, more commercial theatres. For this reason, being an active part of the community was an important part of their remit.

1.4.5 Artistic and education policies

Throughout the interviews and accompanying documentation, many references were made to the theatre companies' policies, both in artistic and educational terms. Words such as 'mission', 'vision' and 'priorities' were frequently used.

In terms of artistic policies, the ten theatre companies in the sample were all relatively clear about their aims and objectives, despite the enormous variety of different aims and objectives attributed to each individual company. Some companies were dedicated to the production of new work, or work of high artistic integrity, others were more concerned with providing an accessible theatre experience. The children's theatre company, and the touring company producing work for young people in youth clubs, were particularly concerned with the educational aspects of their work, whilst still retaining artistic merit. The theatre festival existed specifically to promote the work of international touring theatre companies.

In terms of policies relating specifically to education, there were even clearer differences between the companies in the sample. Of the ten companies, only half had a written education policy document. However, a wide variety of reasons for having no written policy were suggested. Surprisingly, two of the companies where there was no written education policy were those producing work specifically for children and young people. The children's theatre company explained that integration was so fundamentally embedded into their work that education policies were part of their main mission statement. Similarly, in the case of the touring company producing work for young people in youth clubs, education was articulated as a main aim in the management committee report.

It would seem, therefore, that education policies tended not to exist as separate documents in theatres where education was the prime function of the company, and fully integrated into their work. The companies that had separate education policies were clearly those with separate education departments, and an apparent distinction between the core artistic work and education.

Further, more detailed, information about artistic and educational policies and practices can be found in Chapters 2 and 4.

1.4.6 Funding

Theatre company funding was an issue of considerable importance which was raised frequently by interviewees from all the companies in the sample. There were several key sources of funding which were widely accessed.

♦ All of the theatres in the sample mentioned funding directly from the Arts Council, or from their Regional Arts Board. Some referred to a combination of different types of funding from both these sources.

- ♦ Local authorities, local and county councils were another major source of financial support. Only one of the companies – a touring company – did not mention a local authority, and four out of the ten also listed support from one or more county councils.

- ♦ Interviewees from only three out of the ten theatres mentioned their own, earned, income – whether through box office sales, catering, or merchandise, in their financial structure. However, all of the theatre companies' financial reports suggested that they received some income from this source.

In addition, there was a range of other sources exploited by only some of the different companies.

- ♦ The children's theatre company had received a grant from the Lottery which they had used to purchase a new sound and lighting system. One of the regional repertory theatres was also in the process of bidding for a major Lottery grant in order to completely redevelop their building – bringing it up to date with modern facilities and technology.

- ♦ A variety of different funding bodies coming under the broad umbrella of 'charitable trusts and foundations' were listed by interviewees from six of the theatre companies, and a further company was beginning to explore this avenue. In two of the companies, money from these sources was specifically ring-fenced for education work.

- ♦ In a similar way, six companies described sponsorship or donations that they received – again, mostly connected with specific projects, many of which included an education element.

In seven of the theatre companies, some funding specifically for education work and staff was allocated out of the main budgets. Two of the remaining companies considered all of their work to be educational, and therefore considered their entire budget to be for education, rather than setting aside a specific fund. Interestingly, the children's theatre was not one of these two companies – they received money from the core budget to fund the education officer's post and resource development.

However, despite some core budget funding, many of the theatre companies described the need to raise additional money in order to carry out specific education projects. There was substantial resistance to the notion that funding influenced educational aims, or was a factor in the work that was planned and achieved, but in all of the companies it was clear that difficult decisions were being made on a routine basis. At one of the regional repertory theatres, money was clearly a major issue, and although a considerable programme of education work was being undertaken, it was realised that considerably more could be done with a small increase in financial support and security.

1.4.7 The extent of education work

To a certain degree, the extent of the education programmes being offered, and planned, by the theatre companies in the sample was dependent on many of the issues already raised in this chapter. The type, size, funding arrangements and theatre policies or mission were all significant factors. Definitions of what actually constituted education work were also noticeably different from company to company.

All of the ten theatre companies in the sample professed to be, or had been in the past, engaged in some form of education work. However, the extent of that education work varied considerably – from those (such as the children's theatre, the touring company specialising in productions in youth clubs and the rural touring company) who claimed it as their main *raison d'être*, to others where it was clearly a far lesser feature of their activities. Only one (touring) theatre company was not currently providing any educational work, although this was an area they wished to develop in the future.

All of the regional repertory theatres in the sample offered broadly similar types of education programmes – generally including specific youth-orientated performances, resource materials supporting youth performances and main house shows, touring performances to schools, workshops, summer schools, and youth theatre. However, the emphasis was different across the different companies.

1.4.8 Consultation with client groups and advisory support

Consulting with consumers, and potential consumers, on performances and education programmes was clearly a very important activity for many of the interviewees in the sample. However, consultation was often viewed in terms of evaluation of events which had already happened, and using evaluation to inform further work.

One regional repertory company had a very close working relationship with the drama advisory service of the local authority – often producing collaborative work – which was seen to be very beneficial.

In many ways, advisory support was seen by the companies to be very closely associated with the process of consulting their client groups. The client groups were often seen as the best advisers. Only half of the ten companies had specific education advisory groups which met regularly to provide help and advice up-front. In addition, several of those where advisory groups did exist reported difficulties in encouraging people to attend.

Further information about evaluation can be found in Chapter 3, which considers specific education programmes in each of the theatres in the sample.

1.4.9 Training

All of the theatre companies in the sample were able to refer to the education work and programmes which they were delivering (or planning to deliver). However, the backgrounds and training of the people who were engaged in delivering or mediating those programmes varied markedly. Training for theatre education work was, therefore, an issue of acute importance.

Permanent theatre company staff were the most likely to have benefited from training – both in general terms, and specifically for education work. Seven out of the ten theatre companies referred to various different types of training which staff had received – often in response to a staff appraisal system. This included: IT, team leadership, management and marketing.

As already mentioned all of the theatre companies relied heavily on the use of freelance workers – particularly in the mediation of education programmes. The background and training of these freelance workers varied enormously, and in some cases concerns were raised over their abilities – particularly from theatre companies not based in London.

Very few of the freelance workers involved in education work who were interviewed mentioned any training which they had received from the company they were working for. However, some directors and permanent education staff from two of the theatres did provide internal training for their freelance staff, and the touring company specialising in work for young people described the detailed induction process which actors and workshop leaders went through. The key problem with the training of freelance education workers was the finance – who should pay for it. Theatre companies – already working to tight budgets – were generally unwilling to invest in training for a freelance worker who may not work with the company for very long. Conversely, freelance workers were often unwilling to give up their own time to participate. One freelance youth theatre organiser understood the theatre's reluctance to pay for education, and also said that he would expect to be paid for spending time attending a course.

Despite having identified this shortfall in terms of the training of freelance education workers, it was often apparent that the use of freelance workers brought a range of skills and abilities into the theatre companies which permanent staff could then learn from.

1.5   Structure of report

The remainder of this report consists of four chapters:

Chapter 2: The aims of the education programme starts by presenting a typology of the different aims and objectives of education programmes described by interviewees from the different theatre companies. It then describes the change and flexibility of those aims, explores the question of whether all theatre companies should have education programmes, and looks at the distinctive contribution that the theatre can make to education in general terms.

Chapter 3: The design and implementation of theatre education programmes explores the origination of ideas for education projects, the planning and designing of projects, project management and staffing, the target groups, community involvement, and partnerships and collaboration. The chapter concludes with specific examples of education projects from the ten companies in the sample and analyses the ways in which they deliver the various education aims defined in Chapter 2.

Chapter 4: The relationship between the company's education programme and its other activities considers the extent of integration of education work into the core programme, the desirability of integration, and factors influencing the status of education within the company.

Chapter 5: Summary and conclusion summarises the main findings from the research and addresses the fourth of the key aims – raising issues which may inform the development of policy and practices in theatre companies' education programmes.

2. THE AIMS OF EDUCATION PROGRAMMES

2.1 Introduction

During the interviews, company members were asked to describe the company's educational aims and objectives. They were asked whether such aims had changed or developed in any way, and what had influenced any changes. They were also asked whether they believed all theatre companies should provide education programmes, and to identify what they regarded as the distinctive contribution of theatre to education in its broadest sense.

Interviewees' interpretations of 'education' varied, and this was seen to impact directly on the way they conceived their educational aims. One director observed:

We don't have the word 'education' in our artistic aims at the moment, largely because of our positioning in the market-place, that often education is perceived as schools' work, whereas education for me is a much broader thing. The Government are now beginning to talk about lifelong learning and such like, so we see it very much – much more holistic, a broader picture, and we don't – we are not locked into any National Curriculum requirements.

At the same time, companies differed in their views on the value of a written education policy. Only the five companies with separate education departments had a separate written education policy. However, one administrator thought that the education policy had been written '*because the funding bodies required it*' rather than because the company felt it needed to be in writing. An experienced education director elsewhere said he was '*not a great believer in written policy statements*' and alleged that he had never worked with a company which had a written policy. While the majority of companies appeared either to have achieved or to be aiming for consensus on their educational aims, there could also be disagreement on whether a consensus was desirable. One education officer had found that, in his experience, '*when it comes to young people, everyone has an opinion on how to work with them, because everyone has been one, so brings that baggage*'. He regarded this diversity of views as a resource rather than a disadvantage because, '*that's ... part of the point of theatre and especially education work in theatre ... to make people think, to make people argue, to shock people or to anger people or to just excite people really, and that should be for the staff as well as participants*'.

Educational aims were often most clearly articulated by artistic directors, administrators and education officers. Although many freelance workers appeared to have imbibed a company's overall educational commitment, a number of them admitted to limited knowledge of the aims in detail.

As illustrated in the previous chapter, the companies in the sample displayed considerable diversity which emerged in their perceptions of particular educational aims, the respective emphasis ascribed to these aims and the degree to which they were interrelated. One experienced education officer who had been conferring with colleagues in other parts of the country felt that '*each education department has a different slant to it*'. She attributed this to the different '*skills, and experiences and interests of the people that are involved in delivering the work*'. This diversity of approach is clearly demonstrated by the range of educational aims that emerged through analysis.

2.2   A typology of aims

The range of educational aims extended from a state of total integration with a company's artistic aims through a position, where they were carried out as a discrete and subordinate function of the company, to a situation in which they were still at an evolutionary stage because of current management and funding difficulties.

From the plethora of specific aims identified in the data, five broad categories gradually became discernible. It will be seen from the ensuing discussion that the typology does not place these categories in any hierarchical sequence. However, as the following discussion points out, 'Client-centred educational aims' (type D) were the most frequently cited.

A.   Educational aims totally integrated with artistic aims

B.   Drama/theatre-centred educational aims

1.   *To develop practical theatre skills*

2.   *To develop the capacity for critical appreciation of theatre*

   a)   to develop a deeper understanding and appreciation of theatre and dramatic form

   b)   to inform and educate audiences/learners about particular pieces

   c)   to extend knowledge of the historical context of plays/writers

C. Curriculum development and support (proactive)

3. To support teacher education and training

4. To support teachers in their teaching, opening another dimension on work in the classroom

    a) for theatre studies/drama/English lessons

    b) for other areas of the curriculum (literacy/numeracy/history/ PSE, etc.)

5. To provide theatrical performances as a resource for schools

6. To raise the profile of drama in schools

D. Client-centred educational aims

7. Aims related to personal development (especially for young people)

    a) to enrich individual lives and provide enjoyment

    b) to engage the emotions and imagination

        i) in order to explore 'difficult' areas of experience

        ii) in order to open alternative perspectives/challenge the status quo

    c) to offer opportunities for self-expression, physically and orally, in order to develop self-confidence and self-esteem

    d) to offer opportunities for social interaction and teamwork

8. Aims relating to the community (proactive)

    a) to recognise and explore social issues:

        i) cultural diversity

        ii) social inclusion

        iii) lifelong learning

    b) to be a resource for a community in a specific geographic location

    c) to reach out specifically to young people outside school

9. Educational aims tailored to constituents' needs (reactive)

    a) aims responding to school needs

    b) responding to young people's needs in particular

    c) responding to needs of a specific geographic community

E. Aims relating to the needs of theatre companies

10. Educational aims supporting artistic aims

   a)   to contribute to the development of the art of theatre in general

   b)   to provide creative opportunities for theatre artists

   c)   to commission and perform new writing/new music

11. Aims directed towards the survival of theatre companies

   a)   audience development

       i)   *to build audiences for and broaden access to theatrical performances*

       ii)   *to broaden artists' professional development to include training for education work*

       iii)   *to ensure that young people perceive the concept of theatre as relevant (repertoire, venue, marketing, educational approach)*

   b)   to attract funding

12. Dissociation from educational aims

Not applicable to companies here, but validated in reference to companies outside the sample.

The educational aims of most companies included a variety of those listed in the typology. Company members frequently acknowledged that the aspirations relating to the enrichment of understanding and everyday experience, for young people and, in many cases, the wider community, had to be tempered by a recognition of the company's need for financial survival and its artistic viability.

One very experienced artistic director defined three distinct educational aims for his company: ' ... *it's to give the kids who come a better time... to give them an understanding of the play before they see it ... to get a more sophisticated response*'. The company accordingly held workshops for students from schools and colleges before a performance; on another level, he believed that the workshops were '*an aim in themselves*'. Working with a theatre director like himself provided a different educational approach from that of the teacher ... '*about theatre process and how one directs scenes ... how one approaches the text ...*'. On a third level, he said education could be seen as '*a marketing tool*' in terms of audience development, because the company made a point of putting pressure on the theatres where they were working to have '*a price that's accessible to colleges and students*'. In terms of priorities, however, he was convinced that his first aim was the most important. His company's work could be very challenging in terms of form and content – both '*alarming and anecdotal*' and he was committed to '*contextualising it and placing it in a situation where normal people would be able to comprehend it and get a great deal more out of it*'.

Given that, in the case of most companies, educational aims seemed to be interrelated, it would be inappropriate to offer more than a very broad indication of the frequency of their respective occurrence in the data. Client-centred educational aims (type D) appeared to form the dominant group, followed by aims concerned with curriculum development and support (type C) and aims relating to the needs of theatre companies (type E). References to drama, or theatre-centred aims, particularly to specific training in theatre skills, were comparatively muted. *'Dissociation from educational aims'* (type E12) was not applicable to any of the companies in the sample. It appears in the typology because several interviewees recognised its validity in reference to other companies. The following discussion refers to each type of aim from the typology in turn and offers examples from the data.

A. Educational aims totally integrated with artistic aims

Three of the ten companies explicitly embraced the total integration of educational and artistic aims. One artistic director explained *'basically education is, as I say, the mainspring of the whole thing, so it's woven into everything we do, be it the plays, be it the workshops, be it the building, be it the staff, they are all there to communicate with and engage the child, which is educational, you know ...'*. She added that the company increasingly envisaged their *'remit'* to extend beyond their regular work with schools and teachers' panels to *'the wider community'* to encourage children to come to the theatre with their families.

A member of a small-scale touring company was similarly convinced of the fusion of artistic and educational aims in his company's work. As in the previous instance, this approach was embedded in all aspects of the company's daily routine:

> *It's the way in which we answer the telephone, the way in which we engage with someone within the interval of a production ... at its heart, a whole set of other relationships with the communities you work with ... very deliberately not saying 'that's add-on' but saying 'that's part of the same activity'.*

The company's education policy uncompromisingly reflected this view: *'Creating opportunities to learn through the creation of our art is natural to the company's operation.'*

A member of another touring company was equally convinced of the inseparability of the company's artistic and educational momentum. The company specialises in educational work outside schools and do not *'specifically separate'* it from their artistic work. In her view, *'everything we do is informed by young people and informed by their needs, and of course, within that becomes, in its broadest sense an educational objective'*. For her, their education work has to be artistic work *'of the highest quality'* because she feels *'that is what young people deserve'*.

No other companies claimed such total commitment to integration, although for some it was a clearly expressed intention for the future. One interviewee, with considerable experience in and commitment to education work, outlined the problem of making education a priority in a relatively traditional theatre. Currently, '*education is seen in terms of function – operational rather than strategic aims and objectives*'. As he saw it, the location of education in a self-contained department made raising the profile very difficult. The subject of integration will be more fully explored in Chapter 5.

B. Drama-centred education aims

1. ***To develop practical theatre skills***

2. ***To develop the capacity for critical appreciation of theatre***

    a) to develop a deeper understanding and appreciation of theatre and dramatic form

    b) to inform and educate audiences/learners about particular pieces

    c) to extend knowledge of the historical context of plays/writers

As noted earlier, this group of aims was mentioned less frequently than types D (client-centred aims) and E (aims relating to the needs of the theatre company); moreover, there were fewer citations of type B1(to develop practical theatre skills) than of type B2 (to develop critical appreciation).

Some companies explicitly recognised the development of theatre skills as a professional responsibility, and offered work placements and work experience opportunities for students interested in working in theatre. Among the objectives listed in one company's written policy on education and access was the intention of providing '*the highest possible artistic and technical training to young people, thus equipping them if they should choose the arts as a career*'. With reference to an emerging fluidity between art forms, in cross-arts and multi-media work, it may be significant that this company deliberately referred to 'the arts' rather than to theatre alone.

As explained earlier, different educational aims were often perceived to be interrelated. In view of the predominance of client-centred educational aims (type D), it is worth noting that a number of interviewees valued competence in theatre skills not so much for its own sake as for the sense of '*self-empowerment, self-esteem*' which their acquisition bestowed. The producer for a company working with upper secondary school students observed that during '... *the act of making theatre ... there's all sorts of things that can contribute to a young person's development*'. He maintained that such participation can engender enthusiasm for learning in students perceived to be disaffected with the rest of the curriculum, '*bringing forth an attitude to learning which was unsuspected by teachers of any other subject*'. Thus, an ostensibly drama-centred aim was frequently seen to promote a more client-centred aim for personal development.

References to developing the capacity for critical appreciation of theatre (type A2) were more numerous. The importance of '*engaging ... critical skills*', '*to give the kids a better time, to give them an understanding of the play before they see it*' was generally recognised. Companies committed to presenting new and often challenging material were particularly concerned to '*contextualise*' the experience during the preceding workshops in order to '*get a more sophisticated response*'. Placing the play in its historical context was equally important for some companies, those presenting Shakespeare, for example, or plays from the Restoration period.

Again, it may be worth noting that the development of critical skills here, in the first instance for the appreciation of theatre, could also be seen to contribute to the development of a more general capacity for critical analysis and reflection, and thus to be closely related to the personal development aims identified in type D (client-centred aims). The distinctive contribution of theatre to education in this sense will be discussed in the final section of this chapter.

C. Curriculum development and support

3. To support teacher education and training

4. To support teachers in their teaching, opening another dimension on work in the classroom

    a)   for theatre studies/drama/English lessons

    b)   for other areas of the curriculum (literacy/numeracy/history/ PSE, etc.)

5. To provide theatrical performances as a resource for schools

6. To raise the profile of drama in schools

By far the most frequently nominated aim in this category was type C4, 'to support teachers in their teaching', opening another dimension on work in the classroom. Education workers, in particular, emphasised the value of insights into the nature of theatre which could be gained from close collaboration between teachers and theatre artists. Several individuals noted the way theatre companies in schools could bridge the gulf which often existed between the theoretical approach of many teachers and the reality of dramatic interpretation: '*the provision of workshops like this was something that teachers were panting for because they didn't have ... often they came from academic backgrounds not theatrical ones at all ...*'. One interviewee criticised the limited and tokenistic approach to education existing in companies content to reproduce the role of schools in presenting pupils with written materials, instead of providing the unique experience available through working with theatre artists:

> ... *the advantage that theatre has, above the classroom, is it's theatricality, and if an education department is just pumping out*

paper as support material for teachers ... I think it's got to be more sophisticated and innovative than that – that's easy ... we can all get on the internet now, and we can all do that ...

Reluctance to develop contact with schools may, however, be seen as a symptom of the lack of training for education work noted elsewhere in this report. Occasionally, a more cynical view emerged; one observation highlighted the fact that the potential difficulties of working in schools without any educational training could be exacerbated when the schools themselves could offer only minimal commitment. Teachers in his company's locality were *'so overworked'* that he suspected company members had been used as *'supply teachers'*.

Although the majority of comments referred to contributions to curriculum subjects directly concerned with the theatre, some companies were currently engaged with other curriculum areas such as history. An experienced director observed: *'If we're doing a play set on a council estate, it involves, you know, all kinds of departments.'* An education officer referred to the way the company had responded to recent educational reforms with *'quite radical intervention into ... the school curriculum in the climate of literacy, numeracy ...'*, and stressed the importance of arts education in being *'creative in ways of delivery'*.

Providing theatrical performances for schools was an aim which was taken for granted in companies which deliberately conducted their educational activities in formal education. This intention could be seen to be associated with aims concerned with the survival of theatre companies; as explained in the introduction to this section, education could be seen as *'a marketing tool'* in terms of audience development. One chief executive described the *'structured way'* the company had built an *'intensive relationship'* with a *'core umbra of four or five schools'* every year; this policy had *'reaped significant dividends'*.

Among the companies working in schools, expression of the need to raise the profile of drama in schools as an aim *per se* was surprisingly rare. While they acknowledged increasing emphasis in the curriculum on literacy and numeracy, individuals tended to highlight their flexibility in response to such changes, rather than to dwell on their possible repercussions for the status of the arts in schools. One education officer pointed out that the arts certainly could be *'downgraded'* in some schools in favour of academic subjects, but that it was all the more important for theatre companies to be versatile in what they had to offer.

Several companies were actively engaged in professional development activities for teachers. *'Skills-based workshops for teachers'* were identified as one of the practical schemes for promoting *'school ties'* in one company's education policy, and *'workshops for teachers linked to particular productions'* featured in that of another; a third company's policy referred to a *'teacher forum'*. The education officer in this last example drew attention to the importance of *'investing in other people'* entrusted with mediating the company's educational package. Another education worker felt it was very important to stimulate debate, among secondary school pupils during workshops, which could be continued after the company had withdrawn. He said teachers did occasionally write and tell them they still referred to individual workshops in their lessons. Perhaps teachers would be more committed to activities to develop the company's work if they were given more support? Continuity and progression for learners is referred to later (in 3.7.5). The need to equip teachers, as in the examples above, to follow through the work which theatre companies initiate, may be a further aspect of education work for companies involved in work with schools to consider in the future.

D. Client-centred educational aims

In considering what is meant by 'education', it is interesting that there were noticeably more responses under this section than under type C (curriculum development). While all except one company had developed relationships with schools to varying degrees, interviewees across all companies referred to personal development, and to 'community aims', particularly those relating to social concerns. Building-based companies stressed their responsibility as a resource to their 'local' community, however immediate or far-flung that community happened to be (see Chapter 3, 3.9.1). Aware as most interviewees were of the focus of the research, it may be that their responses were weighted consciously or unconsciously towards category D. At the same time, many of them expressed such ardent conviction of the potency of live theatre that such advocacy seems more likely to be a true reflection of their aspirations. Managers and artistic directors were often quite open about the need to be pragmatic in terms of partnerships and funding opportunities, but a steadfast reluctance to compromise on core artistic values, and thus on the distinctive nature of their company's education work, recurred throughout the data, particularly among artistic directors.

---

7. *Aims related to personal development (especially for young people)*

    a)   to enrich individual lives and provide enjoyment

    b)   to engage the emotions and imagination

         i)   *in order to explore 'difficult' areas of experience*

         ii)   *in order to open alternative perspectives/challenge the status quo*

    c)   to offer opportunities for self-expression, physically and orally, in order to develop self-confidence and self-esteem

    d)   to offer opportunities for social interaction and teamwork

---

The analysis of types of aims which follows continues to demonstrate the interrelationship between aims in different categories. The aims of enriching individual lives, and engaging the emotions and imagination, were frequently associated with companies' work in schools. Opportunities for self-expression and for social interaction were also valued as consequences of the development of practical theatre skills, as noted earlier.

Bearing in mind the earlier comments relating to the need to prepare young audiences to appreciate performances to the full, the excitement of experiencing theatre for an individual child, '*to have Twelfth Night ... come alive in front of them*', was widely recognised: '*they'll appreciate it and that's a private thing*'. One interviewee realistically added that '*in a sort of mercenary way*' the hope is that the memory of such excitement would make them want to return, thus associating an altruistic aim with more practical considerations. However, since he appeared content for young audiences to return either '*here*' or to '*any other theatre*', a desire for the welfare of theatre in general, at least in this instance, seemed to override concern for the company's own audience development.

The power of theatre to stir the emotions and imagination, its ensuing potential for confronting controversial issues, and for offering alternative and often challenging perspectives, was vehemently affirmed by many interviewees, particularly members of companies which concentrated on new writing, and on social concerns. One of the biggest priorities, according to a freelance education worker, was '*to stimulate discussion with young people and get them thinking about things ...*' so that '*they can relate those events to their own lives or their peers*'. An actor believed theatre '*should invigorate*' and another interviewee referred to wanting to '*stretch*' audiences of all ages in '*ways* [they] *did not necessarily want to go*'. One director vividly depicted the disquieting emotional charge of theatre and its power to undermine unquestioned assumptions and beliefs:

> *... an emotional response which can't be captured in the National Curriculum, which is about you, for the first time feeling empathy for somebody that you never thought you would, or identifying with a character and realising something about yourself ...*

In terms of personal development, the experience of participation, in workshops and/or through preparing for a performance, was generally very highly rated. Working with others towards individual and collective understanding of a piece of theatre, acquiring direct experience of dramatic form, and competence in relevant skills, was widely held to offer unique opportunities both for self-expression, as a means of nurturing self-esteem and for social interaction and teamwork as a means of promoting cooperation and communication skills. It is worth pointing out that, passionate advocates of theatre as many interviewees undoubtedly were, those who had witnessed the personal benefits for young, and in some cases older, participants frequently regarded personal development as a legitimate aim in itself. An education officer of a regional company with a thriving youth theatre referred to the emphasis the education department put on '*self-expression and self-development*' in their participatory activities. At another regional theatre, the artistic director expressed his determination to develop the company's education work; the intention of building '*confidence and self-esteem*' was specifically identified in the company's written education policy. The administrator of a touring company spoke for many interviewees:

> *I think the participatory theatre is incredibly enriching, liberating ... a way of helping people to develop their own confidence and*

skills, in social situations, in group working, teamwork, that you just don't get in formal education ...

She further suggested that this particular experience was not available in other art forms.

8. *Aims relating to the community (proactive)*

a) to recognise and explore social issues:
- i) *cultural diversity*
- ii) *social inclusion*
- iii) *lifelong learning*

b) to be a resource for a community in a specific geographic location

c) to reach out specifically to young people outside school

The extent to which companies were proactive (D8) or reactive (D9) in formulating aims in relation to their audiences was often difficult to determine. While some had specific target groups in mind, and building-based companies were frequently committed to a specific community, there was general recognition of the need for flexibility, and individuals in several companies alluded to the value of evaluation following education work as a means of keeping in touch with participants' views.

Interviewees across all companies referred to the need to address cultural diversity, although approaches varied considerably: for building-based companies according to where they were located, and for touring companies according to the nature of their touring communities or to their specific target groups. The director of one theatre said it was '*very important*' that the company visited schools where there was a large Asian population; they avoided presenting '*a group of white middle-class actors*' and deployed a racial mix of artists for every production. The education officer of another company referred to the '*very fruitful and vibrant relationships*' which could evolve from blending the work of '*very, very small geographical specific places in London*' with that of international artists '*who of course come from precisely the same sort of places themselves*'.

In the interests of promoting black culture, a small touring company had decided to concentrate on black music theatre. This was partly in order to reach young black audiences, for whom music was perceived to be the most popular cultural medium, and partly to provide creative opportunities for the '*best black artists*', whose talents were perceived to lie in music and performance art. Such a culturally driven approach seems to combine proactive and reactive community aims with the artistic aims of providing creative opportunities for theatre artists.

For companies working in largely monocultural areas, cultural diversity could be a particularly sensitive area. One company member explained that the challenge of presenting multiculturalism, especially to younger audiences, was translated into practice through '*broader policies ... particularly at Christmas when the kids are in ... you are looking at a mixed cast, so you are at least representing society's mix ...*'. The company's education policy referred to the intention to take the lead in fostering audience tastes, and in acquiring '*the knowledge and assurance to deal with the most challenging material*'.

With reference to social inclusion, several interviewees observed that it was necessary to be proactive if you were aiming to extend education work beyond the sphere of traditional participants. An education officer outlined the reasons for changing tactics after setting up a young people's company: '*Applications ... tended to be from the kind of young people who had the means to find out, their parents came to the theatre, they went to schools where theatre was important.*' The crucial role of the development officer of a touring company was building relationships with youth clubs and other youth organisations in touring communities, in order to reach the young people least likely to attend performances at a traditional theatre. Another interviewee spoke of what could be achieved through working in schools for children with learning difficulties and physical disabilities.

From a company hoping particularly to reach '*disadvantaged young people*' in the local community, however, came a note of warning. An education worker noted that it was '*dangerous*' to think that theatre can answer all young people's social problems. She felt that while theatre was good for exploring issues, it is not necessarily a means of resolving them. The oblique reference here to a sense of pressure to take on a social remit was echoed elsewhere; another company felt they were currently '*fighting people off with a stick*' because it was impossible to be '*all things to all people*'.

The consideration of lifelong learning was felt to be important by several companies. An education officer averred it was '*key*' in terms of professional development for young artists (thus linking with artistic aims) and also in terms of providing opportunities for enthusiastic amateurs, as in the theatre's writers' group, who had no professional aspirations. Where Board members worked in higher education institutions, their professional interests were seen to sharpen awareness of lifelong learning in a company's educational objectives.

Building-based companies expressed strong commitment to their local community. One company's policy described their work as a '*central learning resource across the region*'. In addition to a young people's company, they offer a '*People's Company ... drawn from the adult community*', distinguished from '*other local amateur societies*' by its '*learning and developmental structure*'. An education officer of a touring company with a local catchment area referred to work in local communities as '*creating a sense of ownership of the company in a sense of togetherness within the venues that we work ...*'. The value of a potential audience on the doorstep was highlighted by another touring company, which had recently acquired its own base. The company's educational aims had crystallised once the prospect of developing community relationships became a reality. In the words of the artistic director, '*it seemed a key to a new beginning to take the community aspect into account*'.

Although several companies targeted young people outside formal education, for one company it was their overriding aim. Performances in youth clubs and other unconventional community spaces could present additional challenges for the skills of the company members involved. The urgent need for training in this education work recurred throughout the data. On their own ground, young audiences are free to walk away, and to ignore invitations to participate; consequently, the need for relevance of content, communication style and marketing is acutely perceived. As one experienced freelancer explained:

> *You're on their territory, you're on their turf, and I think the work has to be pitched at a certain level.*

Moreover, as another interviewee observed, '*the dynamic of working with young people is always changing*'; sensitivity to the '*ephemeral*' nature of youth culture was held to be of paramount importance.

9. *Educational aims tailored to constituents' needs (reactive)*

  a) aims responding to school needs

  b) responding to young people's needs in particular

  c) responding to needs of a specific geographic community

As explained earlier, interviewees frequently blurred the distinction between 'proactive' and 'reactive' aims in their responses. In terms of responding to school needs, in some cases it might seem almost more appropriate to say that companies were proactive in being reactive. The policy statement of one theatre perceived its main (proactive) objective as '*to create and present dynamic theatre*' for children. The document later testified to a deliberately reactive approach in the way in which they linked their productions to National Curriculum attainment targets, and ensured a close and continuous relationship with their Teachers Advisory Panel, '*which addresses planning and programming and previews each production*'.

One interviewee felt that the National Curriculum had '*changed programming*' and was '*slightly strangleholding the situation*'. For companies aiming to offer young people challenging new material and alternative perspectives on personal and social concerns, responding to curriculum-oriented school needs could sometimes compromise fundamental educational intentions.

One company's education work had '*accelerated*' very rapidly when they decided on an A-level set text for a forthcoming production. By sending out a free workpack to any schools across the country who applied for it, they gained '*a huge database ... a network*' of schools and colleges to build relationships with in the future. The artistic director was keen to point out, however, that this instance of deliberate reactivity was '*exceptional*', and referred to a recent occasion when the company had refused an opportunity for funding which involved running school workshops in London, because the work '*didn't in fact fit in with any play that we were doing*'.

In terms of responding to young people's needs, the policy of a theatre with a well-established education department referred to '*creating channels for feedback for young people*'. This aim was very specifically put into practice by a small touring company. They prioritised young people, and had recognised that access to the internet could certainly not be taken for granted. The kind of young people they were targeting would not necessarily have computers at home, and might not be regular attenders at school. In order to ensure that their education work kept in touch with these young people's needs, they had designed colourful '*chatback cards*' for distribution in youth clubs to elicit details about '*lifestyle, what they do*'.

The practice of responding to the needs of a specific geographic community was universal among companies able to relate to localities in this way. A company with a local remit had collaborated with two other theatres on a summer school for young Asians. The project reflected their fundamental aim of targeting young people unfamiliar with theatre, and company members were enthusiastic about its perceived success. A director of a regional theatre felt the way in which young people were dispersed in residential areas, cut off from the town centre by a ring road, made it harder for them to acquire a sense of belonging to a community. The cultivation of younger audiences was high on his agenda and he was hoping to use the theatre's education work as a means of giving them a '*network*', a sense of community identity.

In some cases, the relation of community aims to funding considerations could be problematic. A member of another theatre also felt links with the surrounding community needed to be determined by the nature of the theatre's particular catchment area, and that an externally agreed set of funding criteria could be inappropriate. He said that, in their reports to sponsors, the company were constantly having to record '*the percentage of projects*' aimed at particular social or ethnic groups, and he felt they could be more effective in meeting local needs if they were left to identify target groups within the community themselves.

E. Aims relating to the needs of theatre companies

10. Educational aims supporting artistic aims

    a) to contribute to the development of the art of theatre in general

    b) to provide creative opportunities for theatre artists

    c) to commission and perform new writing/new music

Artistic aims, and concerns relating to audience development, the shortage of skilled and experienced staff to deliver education work, and the challenge of achieving sustainable relevance for young people, surfaced persistently, if not continuously, throughout the data, as earlier examples of interrelated aims have shown. The perpetual pressures to attract funding, whether for survival in the immediate future, or beyond the period for which the company was currently secure, lurked behind many senior managers' educational aspirations, and also created a sense of instability for freelancers.

Along with more specific artistic aims, a number of interviewees referred to a non-specific aspiration '*to make good art*', to contribute to the development of art, or theatre, in general. The avowed intention was to produce '*artistic work of the highest quality*'. For a community theatre, art had been '*the sacred centre*' throughout its recent history. In a company whose educational aims were undeniably demonstrated to be their *raison d'être*, the work was unhesitatingly perceived to be '*artistically driven*'. Most companies professed equal determination to innovate and to experiment. One interviewee defended his company's right to work '*inspirationally*'; an actor elsewhere portrayed his company's recent productions as '*adventurous*' in '*breaking new ground*'.

Education work could open up creative opportunities for individual artists. A Board member emphasised the importance of increasing younger artists' confidence to '*do their own thing, develop their own aesthetic, which is not derived from commercial sources*'. A key figure in one company was a composer, and the decision to produce music theatre, primarily to appeal to their targeted audience, was also valued for the possibilities involved not only for him, but for a developing network of other musicians and performance artists.

Commissioning and performing new writing were an aim to which many companies subscribed. In some cases, this artistic aim was as yet largely unrealised, but in others it underpinned every production, simultaneously fulfilling general educational aims by exploring personal experience, challenging accepted perspectives, and/or examining social or cultural concerns. An education worker in one company explained their work was '*predominantly contemporary new work*'. Elsewhere, an interviewee who believed that '*learning is integral in story*' asserted that '*commissioning new writing*' for children was one of the company's strengths. Several companies specified new writing as a priority in their documentation.

---

11. ***Aims directed towards the survival of theatre companies***

   a)   audience development

      i)   *to build audiences for and broaden access to theatrical performances*

      ii)   *to broaden artists' professional development to include training for education work*

      iii) *to ensure that young people perceive the concept of theatre as relevant (repertoire, venue, marketing, educational approach)*

   b)   to attract funding

In terms of audience development, unanimous concern was expressed for *'the theatre to go on living'*. One interviewee drew attention to the importance of keeping abreast of *'technological'* advances in the presentation of performances, perhaps especially pertinent where young people are concerned. A freelance producer expressed awareness of the temptation to subordinate education as a vehicle for audience development; she upheld that the company she was involved with saw education and audience development as part of the same thing and she believed that the anticipated appointment of a *'dedicated'* education officer would enable them to see this philosophy through. The priority was *'to use the company as a resource for the kids rather than the other way round'* and she cited the company's annual music festival as a recent example.

The paucity of provision for training for education work was recorded earlier in this report. Interviewee perceptions of their own proficiency in education work, and that of the freelancers they employed, varied considerably. One individual asserted that compared with a few years ago, when she felt her company was *'pioneering a style of participant-centred education'*, some practitioners had now acquired some *'very good experience'*. Significantly, she believed her own *'creative learning'* had been enhanced through collaboration with others. However, many other interviewees expressed frustration at the constraints imposed by a lack of adequately trained education workers. Referring in the first instance to restrictions on education programmes due to funding, one interviewee pointed out that *'it's not just money ... it's also the availability of the right qualified staff'*.

The feeling across all companies was that young people were as entitled as any other section of the population to experience art of the highest quality. Most companies also appeared to be aware that appealing to younger audiences demanded explicit recognition of both their culture, in terms of interests and tastes, and of their preoccupations, in terms of age and social context. Some, however, had gone further than others in putting these perceptions into practice. One individual stressed the importance of *'having a story ... good characterisation and complex characters, complex emotions and not being afraid of addressing that ...'*. She also believed in *'not skimping'* on production values: *'why should that be any less for children?'* By contrast, an interviewee elsewhere admitted to anxiety that companies working in schools, as his company did, were associated with an artform located exclusively within the curriculum: *'kids see us as work'*. He suggested that consequently young people may not see theatre as relevant to their lives outside school: *'No one goes in and teaches them clubbing ... how to go out and have fun on a Saturday night.'* In his view, relating theatre to the National Curriculum may, therefore, be counter-productive to inspiring their enthusiasm. In order to make one regional theatre more relevant to young people's culture, an experienced education worker envisaged major changes in the venue itself, including a *'drop-in space'* with cafes and bars, where the design and atmosphere would be more welcoming and appealing than a traditional foyer.

The relentless pressure to secure adequate funding, in order to operate effectively artistically, and also to provide good-quality education programmes, recurred throughout the data. Some interviewees thought the situation had improved since a few years ago, when, in their view, numerous theatre companies felt they had to offer education work in order to survive. However, many educational aspirations were overshadowed by funding anxieties. In the case of one theatre, restricted funding was seen to affect the extent of the education work they could offer. Although the director was very keen to do more '*outreach work*', they currently lacked the resources to forge links beyond a limited number of schools. The administrator of a company specialising in music theatre noted that music itself incurred extra expenditure, in terms of production costs. This company depended heavily on the success of current funding applications to reach their chosen target group.

Companies which had fixed-term funding from the Arts Council were required to provide education and outreach by funding agreements. One such agreement referred to the company's commitment to seek funding for an 'Outlook' director. A company member explained how sponsorship from a charity had influenced their educational aims by expecting them to access '*young people in poor areas*' in particular. This in turn was seen to increase the pressure to ensure that education workers received appropriate training, to equip them to communicate sensitively with a potentially challenging target group. Companies with local authority funding were expected to be energetic in their links with the community. In one case, the local council was on the one hand pressurising the company to '*cut costs and streamline everything*' but on the other hand, as a specific funding provider, was putting the company under pressure to achieve mutually established targets: '*there are promises that we have to live up to.*' Obligations like this were sometimes seen as in danger of taking precedence over a theatre's prime artistic function. The comments of one or two interviewees reflected the findings of an earlier Arts Council Report on theatre companies, which suggested that some local authorities may '*fund for added value rather than from a commitment to drama as art*' (Peter Boyden Associates, January 2000).

In many cases, however, in spite of a realistic acknowledgement of the often time-consuming task of negotiating with funders, the determination not be deterred from their fundamental artistic mission was forcefully expressed. One director cited examples of the company's reaction to organisations offering funding for projects. As far as he was concerned, quality came first: '*The reason we do them is "can we do them? Can we do the work well?".*' The proactive approach of a director elsewhere demonstrated a similar sense of purpose: '*We commission and tour new work. We decide what we're going to do and then try and find funding for it so we're not funding led.*'

12. Dissociation from educational aims

Several interviewees acknowledged that there are a number of theatre companies who '*refuse*' to do education work because it does not appeal to them. Although none of the companies in the sample were eligible for this category, they registered awareness and acceptance of companies that were.

The preceding discussion of the typology has analysed the diversity of educational aims professed by theatre companies in the sample, and explored the way in which these aims are frequently interrelated. Reference has already been made to the fact that aims for some companies have changed over time, for various reasons. The following section will outline influences on educational aims in companies where changes were perceived to have occurred. The final two sections will consider, firstly, interviewees' views on whether all companies should offer education programmes and, secondly, their perceptions of the distinctive role of theatre in relation to education.

2.3 Change and flexibility

Members of every company acknowledged changes in educational aims in recent years. Those individuals who denied any changes defined fundamental aims in very general terms. '*The aims of the three 'e's ... to entertain, educate and enthral, the magic of theatre*' was a typical example. Underlying intentions as broad as these were seen to remain constant, alongside a diversity of more specific changes. The speaker here, for example, later referred to the company's response to educational reforms, and also to '*multiculturalism*', which they were committed to '*reflect*' in their education work.

2.3.1 Major changes in the company's mission

Some of the smaller companies had experienced a radical reappraisal of their overall mission. Those which had identified themselves as '*part of the alternative theatre movement of the 'sixties*' had needed to '*shift*' their '*sense of purpose*' to survive; by the 1990s '*the world was changing very rapidly round them*' and it was a question of '*change or go*'. Redefining the company, and reorienting the artistic mission, had been a valuable opportunity for sharpening the focus on education.

The development of opportunities for collaboration

In the case of one company, a very specific event had propelled them into unprecedented concentration on education work. Unlike other companies involved with schools, which claimed to have responded assiduously to the National Curriculum, the decision to produce an A-level set text was claimed to be '*exceptional*'. This, however, had resulted in a '*watershed*' for the company's educational work, because the response from schools had been overwhelming and had prompted them to be much more proactive in developing links with new potential audiences.

The peculiar status of non-building-based companies in itself could determine a company's educational aims in a situation where '*audience loyalty was harder to develop*'. One administrator explained that his company's solution had been to '*build up a brand*', an identifiable style which would become a means of identifying with the disparate communities it served. One interviewee reported that the need to forge partnerships, initially as a means of compensating for their lack of a permanent building, had generated a network of contacts across the capital which spawned further opportunities as their reputation for education work had grown. The acquisition of a permanent building, theirs '*for good*', had suddenly directed another company's attention towards the potential of links with a specific community.

Closer association with specific geographic communities, through the acquisition or enlargement of premises, through local funding partnerships or other collaboration with local organisations, was believed to be a highly significant influence on educational aims in a number of companies. The degree to which companies were influenced by their perceived constituents was discussed in section D of the typology above. More will be said about partnerships in the following chapter.

The commitment of the chief executive

The commitment of the chief executive, often the artistic director, emerged as crucial, '*the biggest single factor*', according to one administrator, in ensuring educational aims were translated into practice. The enthusiasm of an effective leader was claimed to permeate the rest of the organisation. An experienced freelance education worker in one company regarded the new artistic director as '*more committed*' than previous occupants of this post. He implied that the limited nature of the education work there was partly due to earlier directors' lack of involvement.

The role of the Board

The Board appeared to influence educational aims in some companies more than others. In one company, the director claimed the Board had no influence whatever on the education policy, while in another an education officer estimated that only about half of the Board understood the implications of education work. By contrast, in a company where the Board included a majority of individuals interested in education, their '*individual critical faculties*' were appreciated as a valuable resource. Elsewhere, Boards were perceived to be '*very supportive*' but too preoccupied with funding considerations to '*sit down and discuss education*'. One company, where the work of a rather isolated education department was seen to be '*operational*' rather than '*strategic*', had recently restructured the Board in order to give the education department more status. There were now five subcommittees, the most central and important of which was that concerned with '*Art, Education and Culture*'. Their purpose, according to the artistic director, was '*not to dictate programming, or inform any of the activities that are done, but to be a sounding board at the highest level – about what the priorities and pressures are*'.

Effective communication

A '*shared understanding*' of educational aims across the company appeared to be affected by a company's size. One interviewee observed that it was '*harder to communicate ... core values*' once a company had '*grown*'. Unanimity over educational aims was more frequently discernible within smaller companies, and several individuals drew attention to the difficulty of maintaining '*actual personal relationships*' when a company was large enough to split into separate departments.

Regional Arts Boards

The importance of Regional Arts Boards (RABs) in the development of educational aims appeared to vary according to perceptions of the opportunities available. In one company, cultural diversity and youth culture were held to '*feed*' their education work more than any initiatives from their RAB. They had been able to use RAB funding for a recent education programme but maintained that the idea for the programme had come first, as a way of fulfilling their educational aims in response to perceived needs in the local community. By contrast, another company had sought an '*intimate relationship*' with their local RAB as a means of creating '*a sense of place and purpose*'.

Media influences

The significance of the media in promoting educational aims often appeared to be negligible. However, interviewees' perceptions seemed to depend on how they interpreted the question. One director said his company was irrelevant to the media, while another interviewee volunteered that it had been '*very nice*' to appear in a major educational newspaper but that this attention had never been followed up. A third individual, however, referred to media influence on the content of the company's productions, and believed that in drawing attention to controversial issues and social concerns, the media had had a considerable effect on the development of plays they had commissioned.

Funding constraints

The impact of funding constraints on educational aims was referred to in section E11 of the typology. One administrative director commented that outreach work connected with a specific production had so far seemed too expensive in terms of freelancers. Another member of the company pointed out that although they were keen to extend education work into '*poorer*' communities beyond their immediate catchment area, this would probably be impossible unless it was subsidised, because the schools concerned would find it '*very difficult to pay*'. Several companies were deterred from attempting to extend their education work to '*underprivileged kids who are not part of the formal education service*' by the current nature of funding agreements.

One interviewee, whose company was already committed to '*quality, long-term relationships with schools*', was frustrated in her aspirations to reach out to young people outside school because the company's wider aims could not be fitted into '*that particular funding stream*'. She echoed the comments of many others when she argued for freedom in the deployment of funding:

I don't want the funding bodies to think up schemes or themes or any of that. I think if we are given the money we will come up with the projects. We should be thoroughly judged and assessed on the success of these projects and the value for money and all the rest of it ...

The preceding discussion has attempted to indicate the diversity of influences on the educational aims of theatre companies, and the changes they have introduced in order to perpetuate both artistic and educational viability and the degree of flexibility required, for an appropriate response to external pressures. Before moving on to a consideration of views of the role of theatre in education, the current section on change and flexibility returns briefly to the implications of a single strand of perceptions which reappeared throughout the data, and which highlighted significant issues concerning education work with young people.

The potential of long-term funding

In terms of inspiring young people with more than fleeting enthusiasm, the need for long-term funding was implicit in the comments of many company members. The following considerations emerged for funders:

♦ **Real change takes time**

In order to bring about any real change in young people's attitudes to theatre, education programmes need to be sustained over a period of time – to allow relationships to develop, ideas to be assimilated and preconceptions to be dispelled. Instilling a deeper and more long-lasting interest than mere novelty value requires a commitment to continuity and progression. *'One-off'* events were generally regarded as ineffective in terms of engaging more than temporary enthusiasm.

♦ **Training**

Appropriate training was seen as paramount in order for artists to mediate effective education programmes, and in order for education work to be a positive rather than a demoralising experience for the artists concerned. Some artists and managers see education work as a valuable opportunity for staff development. However, a continuing programme of induction and good-quality training has to be reliably resourced.

♦ **Sensitivity to young people's culture**

The ephemeral quality of youth culture means adaptability is essential if companies are to be able to respond effectively to young people's needs and expectations. Moreover, traditional venues are often seen by young people as unwelcoming, unappealing and unsympathetic to their own culture. Theatres need to try to diminish the sense of elitism perceived by many young people *'who think that theatre is ... posh – red seats, velvet curtains ...'*, and to demonstrate that theatre is relevant to young people's lives.

♦ **Risk-taking**

Risk-taking was seen as integral to good-quality education programmes – companies need to be supported to withstand the continuing element of uncertainty involved in working with young people. Potential risks were perceived, for example, in the experience of the creative process itself, in commissioning new writers, in working in unconventional settings, and in reaching out to untried target groups.

In addition to long-term funding, many interviewees contended that greater flexibility in funding arrangements would enable them to be more creative, and more effective, in achieving their educational goals.

2.3.2 Should all theatre companies have education programmes?

This interview question evoked a wide range of responses, with different individuals within the same company sometimes expressing alternative points of view. Interpretations of education varied, and very few interviewees gave unqualified answers. One artistic director distinguished between two different types of education programmes:

♦ those which are directly related to the school curriculum; and

♦ those where education is '*not formal, not restricted to young people, not about qualifications, where it is about understanding*'.

In his view, all theatres should have education and 'understanding' at the centre of what they do – '*theatre, above all, helps us make sense of the world*' – but, at the same time, he was not convinced that every theatre company needed a specific department to fulfil a curriculum responsibility.

A freelance actor and workshop leader felt that both participation and performance were equally important from an educational point of view; he thought theatres should always allow their education departments to present performances: there should be '*a product there that children can reach out and appreciate as well as a series of interactive ventures ...*'. Unless education activities led to a performance, he believed, the whole process '*short-changes*' the children involved.

In terms of agreement or disagreement with the expectation to provide education programmes, interviewees' perceptions were fairly evenly spread. Members of companies where education was most closely integrated with their artistic aims did not necessarily believe that every theatre company should have an education programme. Members of one such company felt that any education work was better than none at all because '*learning should be integral in whatever arts you are doing*'. A member of another company, however, where the educational and artistic aims were claimed to be inseparable, gave three reasons why an expectation for all companies to produce education work might be counter-productive:

Because you are kind of imposing things on them that a) they may not be very good at, b) they don't want to do, and c) is in conflict with their artistic intention.

The danger that in these circumstances some companies might only be paying '*lip service*' to education, offering it '*for the wrong reasons, the wrong pressures*', was noted by a number of interviewees. One workshop leader, who supported the inclusion of education work, contributed '*a very strong proviso*' that a company should not merely '*provide*' it, but '*frame it as part of the core of what they are about*'.

Whether interviewees believed that every company should be involved in education or not, awareness of the need for a coordinated approach, and whole-hearted commitment from the '*apex of the hierarchy*' prevailed throughout the responses. Ideally, it seemed, many individuals would like to see education work happening in theatre companies as a matter of course. But it was widely recognised that education work could only be effective in companies where it was closely aligned with their core artistic purpose, and where those responsible for its delivery were enthusiastic about their work and adequately prepared for its demands.

2.3.3 Theatre's distinctive contribution to education

The invitation to define theatre's distinctive contribution to education yielded a rich abundance of responses, expressed with unmistakable conviction. Although these perceptions reflected the full range of aims referred to in the typology, the client-centred educational aims identified under category D (personal development, and aims relating to the local or wider community) were notably conspicuous.

Perceptions of the special qualities of theatre education related to the following:

◆ **communication through emotion and/or the imagination to challenge preconceptions, and to extend and enhance understanding of ourselves and others**

According to one interviewee, theatre:

... makes us better citizens, it makes us more articulate, it makes us see outside the square – so we view different worlds, different cultures, different people. The plays on stage show us things that we wouldn't otherwise see. It takes us into emotional areas and emotional languages, and that great buzz-phrase 'emotional intelligence' that we wouldn't otherwise encounter. It civilises us.

Theatre's capacity as an '*open forum ... non-judgemental*' was stoutly defended. An artistic director referred to '*a different kind of truth*' uniquely available to the medium of theatre through the resources of emotion and imagination. Many individuals confirmed that active involvement in theatre with members of the profession opened an exciting new dimension on the experience of theatre in the curriculum. A freelance writer claimed live theatre is '*the most concrete*' of all the arts – '*real people, in real space, in real time*', and as such is the most accessible form of communication for addressing anything relating to '*the human condition*'.

♦ **a source of opportunities for self-expression which empowers individuals: and generates self-esteem by allowing them to take risks, and to release 'potential creativity'**

There was widespread acknowledgement of the special power of participation in theatre activities to nurture self-esteem, particularly in relation to young people. It '*creates a safe place ... for those kind of things to happen*', which for some young people may not be available anywhere else. One education worker explained '*you can be whoever you want to be, when most young people are trying to work out who they should be*'. The sense of '*ownership*' of an artform, in the acquisition of specific theatre skills, was also seen as valuable in this respect.

♦ **A collective/community artform**

For a number of company members, it was the '*collective*' which distinguished theatre from other artforms. One director believed that the '*strength*' of theatre was the fact that it was '*predominantly a collaborative experience*' which meant it required '*certain attributes in terms of tolerance ...*'. Another claimed that the sense of collective, shared understanding experienced by being part of a theatre audience was different from experiencing cinema, television or the visual arts. He saw the latter as more individual experiences. His meaning here in relation to the first two may refer to the '*concrete*' quality conferred by the presence of live actors as depicted above. With reference to the visual arts, the individual usually has greater control over the pace of the experience of being a spectator, and this contributes to making its interpretation more personal. In the performing arts, cinema and television, this is not the case, and thus the experience of the audience may be more intense. Another interviewee was more specific about theatre's role as a '*community activity*' – '*you can't make theatre without an audience, you can paint a painting*' – but in theatre, '*nothing happens without an audience*'. Moreover, he identified the inclusiveness of theatre as an artform: '*anyone can contribute*' because it offers such a wide range of opportunities; '*you might not be able to speak*', but making theatre had the potential to involve individuals in some kind of activity whatever their levels of experience, or ability.

The predominance of '*client-centred educational aims*', that is, personal development and closer relationships with the community, is reinforced by perceptions of the distinctive educational contribution of theatre presented here. Stenhouse's vision of lifelong learning – '*a personal and emotive process rooted in culture ... its potential as a source of individual liberation and empowerment*' – may seem particularly apposite in the context of company members' own perceptions of its educational possibilities.

2.4 Summary

According to the preceding analysis, the educational aims of theatre companies offer a picture of considerable complexity, where diverse intentions may be interrelated, a fact in itself acknowledged by several interviewees. In three of the companies, the educational aims were felt to be inseparably integrated with the company's artistic aims, and interviewees in several other companies expressed such integration as a long-term goal. However, according to the typology, 'client-centred' aims, both proactive and reactive, emerged undeniably as an overriding preoccupation, with notably more citations than either curriculum-centred aims (curriculum development and support) or those concerned with theatre companies' artistic and financial survival. References to aims encouraging awareness of the theatre as an artform *per se*, particularly to specific training in theatre skills, were comparatively muted.

In considering such emphasis on personal development and community aims, it may be worth bearing in mind that interviewees may have been more inclined to dwell on their aspirations in this respect by their knowledge of the explicit focus of the research as a whole on education. However, the close association between 'client-centred' aims and the interpretations of theatre's distinctive contribution to education, articulated in the previous section, would seem to support the notion that such aims prevail in the companies' educational approach.

In translating educational aims into practice, there was widespread concern at the restrictions seen to be imposed by a shortage of adequately trained education staff and also by the nature of current funding arrangements. Funding from various sources had enabled all ten companies to develop their education work. However, many senior managers advocated a greater degree of flexibility from sponsors. They argued that this would considerably enhance their ability to generate a continuing and progressive education programme. With greater freedom in the deployment of funding, they believed they would be able to provide education programmes which were in line with both their educational and artistic priorities, and which were also appropriate for the needs of their particular constituencies.

In a review of the current education activities of the companies in the sample, the following chapter will consider the implementation of their respective educational aims with reference to a particular project from each company in turn.

3. THE DESIGN AND IMPLEMENTATION OF THEATRE EDUCATION PROGRAMMES

3.1 Overview

Interviewees were invited to describe a recent education project undertaken by their organisation. The examples described here are therefore illustrations of what interviewees wanted to share, and may not be fully representative of the overall output of each case study theatre company. These may, therefore, be the project of which they were most proud, or perhaps those which they believed would be most valued as examples by others. Interviewees were questioned in detail about aspects of the origin, aims, design and planning of projects, their staffing, structure and content and their relationship to the company's core programme.

While many companies claimed that all of their work was educational (either citing *education as their core activity*, or *education at the core of their activity*), only one of the companies chose to describe a performance with no element of participation by the target group. However, seven of the other projects did have performance as a key element, and four of them involved performance by the target group. One was expected in the future to lead to a performance by the target group, but not for some time.

Of the ten projects described here, five could be said to be 'one-off' projects, devised in order to fulfil the aims and creative ambitions of the companies, or in response to expressed or perceived needs from client groups, and usually both. The other five largely adhered to patterns previously established by each company, but with the content changing in each manifestation. Many projects were regarded by their originators as radical, original or unique, but there seemed to be a lack of awareness of what was happening elsewhere of a similar nature in the field. One company cited a format believing that it was common in many theatres, and indeed one other company did refer to such a model, but this awareness of the coincidence of models was the exception. This may indicate a lack of opportunity to explore the work of other companies.

The scale of educational projects varied enormously, in the numbers of artists and target participants, in the funding allocated, and in the duration. For some, education projects made up the majority of their activity (although the definition of what constitutes an education project can be problematic), while others showed great dedication to a more limited investment in education activities. All would willingly have undertaken considerably more education work if funding permitted, but some were cautious lest education dominated the overall artistic mission. Others were aware that it was even more difficult to obtain funding for the generation of art *per se*, without which education work would be rendered meaningless.

Target groups were very varied. Only two of the projects described below were aimed exclusively at schoolchildren, although four others included schoolchildren as their target audiences or participants. Three were deliberately intergenerational, two were specifically for the youth sector, and reception classes to senior citizens groups were involved.

In describing the distinctiveness of their own educational output, many interviewees claimed the quality of their work as a distinctive feature. Had they been describing particular qualities, this might have been more logical, but to claim a distinctiveness that implied higher quality than elsewhere revealed a laudable pride in their own work, but possibly an ignorance of other work taking place around them. In one case study, two interviewees forcefully stated that there was nothing distinctive about their education work.

3.2 The origination of project ideas

3.2.1 Who has the idea?

The most frequent source of education project ideas was the members of the company itself, or more specifically, the permanent staff. One example was given of the Chief Executive of a large regional repertory theatre, together with an associate artistic director of the company, hatching an initial idea together. In smaller organisations, it was not at all unusual for the artistic director to initiate a project, especially where the core activity of the company was more directly related to young people, education or community development. Education officers were often cited as originating the ideas, but often in response to an artistic programme already defined by the artistic director:

> *The majority of them are me and a drink and fitting in whatever time I can to read whatever has been programmed in the main house. For a long time I was on my own in the department with a team of freelancers ... well, I was the only one in the office, so there was no one to sit and talk about ideas with really. The artistic director and I do talk whenever we can and try and jointly programme, but we are both incredibly busy, so the chances you get to do that are very, very slim.*

(Generally speaking, but with some notable exceptions, the education director had less involvement in the overall artistic programming.) In one case, a marketing director was very central in developing one project into a subsequent one, having spotted an audience development potential, which clearly fitted with the company's aim of extending its clientele.

Freelance contracted artists were less likely to originate ideas, even though they were very widely used for the mediation of projects. This was presumably because they were not an enduring presence, for example when planning was happening. In one case, a freelance education specialist was credited with originating a form of drama workshop, and then adapting it to a different text each year. One company cited occasions when a writer, having an ongoing relationship with the company, had suggested project ideas. Otherwise, freelance artists, whether actors, musicians, designers, etc, seemed to have few opportunities to propose projects. This may well be because they did not usually develop a close and enduring relationship with one company, and were therefore rarely privy to overall planning processes. In one company, where a freelance worker had become a central player in the education work over a few years, there was concern that he could not afford to stay with the work because the uncertain and low level of remuneration might drive him to find more secure work elsewhere.

3.2.2 The stimuli for ideas

Contextual factors

Most companies claimed that ideas stemmed from the need to fulfil their own aims. However, stimuli could come from a variety of sources. As one artistic director put it,

> *I mean they come as a response to a particular question that's troubling ... again it's me ... but I'm not a democrat in that sense, I think that's what happens ... and again I think you will have to test it with others, that if people know they can convince me of an argument, I will listen, I'm a good listener. In the end I suppose most of the work comes as a my kind of response to a particular set of questions.*

Some ideas came as a response to the external context. For example, one company chose to run a theatre training course for young people of South Asian origin, because they realised that there was a dearth of trained young Asian actors available to cast. Another chose to create a rural touring piece in order to fulfil the needs of the community in a recently acquired extension to its touring area.

Funding availability

While most companies were at pains to stress that they did not create work in order to attract funding from outside sources, it would appear that the availability of funding could be a significant factor in the conception of project ideas. One company was asked to do a piece on the issue of arson, and did so because they could justify it in terms of their own aims.

> *The fire service came to us and said, 'Look, we have a statutory responsibility to do work in schools to do with fire; can you do something with us?' And I, kind of, was a bit dismissive and I said 'Do you know how much that sort of work will cost? Every single school in [the county] ... you're looking at £20,000', and*

his response was 'Who should we write the cheque out to?'. So once we'd teased what it was looking for, it was something closer to. Well, first of all he wanted the community involved, which we were instantly interested in, not just young people, so we looked at PTAs, we looked at Governors meetings. The brief was more looking at where does the school sit within the community, as a resource for the community? Well, clearly within rural communities many of whom have secondary schools attached to them, you know, sort of thing. That is a real issue: does this school kind of live here or is it part of the community? So we were up for that, and other people have come to us [insurance company], *who have just asked us to do a bit of work, which was about arson and combating arson, and we were ... it was too agenda based.*

Another company wanted to create a piece to mark the millennium, and it was questionable whether the project could have proceeded without some Millennium Commission seeding money. In some cases, it was a fine point as to whether the idea came first or the knowledge of the possibility of enabling funding. This is a significant factor in that most education projects seem to depend on the ability to attract at least some funding over and above the company's core budget. For at least two companies, the annual repeating of projects, albeit with adaptations and development, was regarded as necessary in order to fulfil the requirements of local funding sources: in other words, an expectation to continue to deliver a particular line of work had been established, at least in the minds of the companies themselves. (The perspectives of funders were not part of this research.)

Response to demand

Two projects were cited in which requests from client groups directly contributed to the initiation of projects. In one case, teachers asked for a Shakespeare production for middle school pupils, and the company then selected the particular play to offer.

There had been lots and lots of requests to put on a Shakespeare play, but not just to go and see a Shakespeare at another theatre, but to actually do it here, specifically for children, so it was programmed in, and again with the teacher advisory panel advising us, and various other ... looking at the curriculum, what would be good to do.

In another, a community, having had a good experience through their children working at school with artists, asked what was going to happen next. This encouraged the company to generate a progression from the original engagement. In both cases, the requesters had already had positive experiences with the companies concerned. In such cases, it could be argued that the companies were responding to the responses of their client groups. More than one interviewee expressed caution about acceding to client demands. The main reasons given were that clients, especially in education, tended to request projects that were more about teaching than about art, and that part of the value of theatre inputs was that they were a surprise to the clients – although this may not always have been regarded as a valued factor by some clients! Another interviewee felt that the education sector was acquiring too much support at too low a price.

We potentially have a problem with the teachers; they are so overworked. So in the end they would love us to work ... to a certain extent, they have been using us, I suspect, as supply teachers.

3.3 Planning and designing projects

3.3.1 Who plans and designs projects?

In many cases, once the idea for a project had been agreed, the originators proceeded with the planning and design of the project. For example, one artistic director, having chosen to run a series of workshops on a particular production, proceeded to devise the material, train other company members in its delivery, and present many of the workshops himself. In another, the artistic director had the initial idea, and almost immediately handed over the development process to the education director, while continuing to '*maintain a kind of vision of it*'. In two other examples, the artistic director quickly brought the directors of partner organisations into the planning process. They devised partly through discussion, and partly by assuming responsibilities for different aspects of the work, and subsequently handed the detailed design of the project to the freelance artists they contracted to mediate the work.

The role of freelance artists seemed to be crucial in much of the planning and design of projects. They were frequently brought in for their specialist expertise in devising, and in some cases then passed the responsibility to execute projects directly to other freelance artists.

3.3.2 Planning during delivery

A most important factor in the planning and design process was the duration of projects. Some were designed and planned to be replicated many times, such as workshops to accompany the run of a particular production, but long-term, one-off participatory projects required ongoing planning, which might involve deliverers and managers. In one case, a project coordinator was employed for 15 months to oversee the development of work leading up to a community production. In some cases, this ongoing planning also needed to involve the funders, who may have been funding on a staged basis, or who needed to be involved in agreeing changes to aspects of the original proposal.

3.3.3 Planning techniques

A favoured method of planning and design involved the originators, along with key developers and/or mediators, spending a period of time together 'workshopping' ideas. This was particularly the case where projects were conceived as a package involving the creation of a new production with educational elements integral to it. It might involve a freelance writer, performers, a designer or a musician. In one case, it occurred some time before the writer delivered a script, and therefore posed availability problems for some freelance workers. However, the specialist expertise of many freelance artists appeared to be a highly valued element in the development process. On the other hand, training of the mediators to undertake some of the educational processes was an element that became more important in situations where a succession of freelance workers was used, and where they were operating as actors (for which they were trained) and workshop leaders (for which they were not).

> *In the old days, actors used to ... there were a whole pool of actors that used to be core company members, who would be employed by the company on a long contract and they would become very skilled up at working with young people, and there would be a whole skills base.*

Although some companies developed longer-term relationships with some freelancers, obviating the need for a complete training process, the freelance field was very fluid overall.

3.3.4 Recycling plans

Some project planning could be described as formulaic, picking up a tried and tested structure and fitting new artistic material into it. In one case, the freelance deviser of the original manifestation continued to plan the specific project for each year, and in the latest version was able to make fairly fundamental changes to the format while remaining true to the original concept. In another case, it would appear that the design remained fairly constant, with the content changing, but there is no reason to assume that this was either more or less appropriate than other approaches.

3.4   How are projects managed?

3.4.1 Management by permanent staff

Not all companies employed an education officer, for a variety of reasons. Even where there was one in post, they may not manage all education projects. Their own skills and experience may mean that they were involved in the delivery of some projects and not others, and they also had the responsibility of overseeing the overall education programme of the company. Some project management required very specialised skills, and some projects were so time consuming that it was inevitable that another, often freelance, person be called in to manage, usually answerable to the education officer, but sometimes to another member of the company management team. Otherwise, projects were normally managed by a permanent member of staff.

In one company, the artistic director played the central role in managing the programme of workshops which was offered to accompany touring productions. This involved maintaining the lists of bookings, contacts and comments and keeping a close eye on the scheduling of workshops. The director's PA then handled the administrative aspects of bookings.

In another, the theatre's administrative director was directly involved in the management of education projects, having assumed that responsibility when the company was very much smaller, relinquished it to a community director for some years, and then resuming it when the financial situation meant losing the community director post. Again, administrative functions were handled by the theatre's general administration staff.

3.4.2 Shared management

Several companies described projects that were run in partnership with other theatre or arts organisations. In those cases, different aspects of management tended to be shared between the various parties, with the initiating company taking a coordinating role.

Another company distributed the management role for different projects amongst the management team, calling the role 'producer'. In the case of a long-term, evolving project, the producer might then refer matters back to the team for discussion and significant decision making. The same company also placed some project management in the hands of a semi-permanent freelance worker, with whom there was a long-term relationship.

Well [the freelance coordinator] *is directly managing it ... I sort of describe her role as a bit like a translator: she moves between the artists and the teachers, between management, between* [the company] *and whatever. But it comes back here because our marketing director is very closely involved as part of how we're relating and discussing things with audiences and potential audiences and this whole business of, you know, longer term.*

3.4.3 Management by freelance workers

Some projects are managed by one-off freelance workers. One company took on a project coordinator for almost 18 months, knowing that it would require a time commitment beyond the capacity available within the staff. The education officer played a support role, while concentrating on other pressing development issues. The education officer then had a brief experience of dispensability.

I became, kind of, advisory. I thought I would be needed more and I actually cleared my desk for the spring to get more involved, but actually it all became rather under control ... it was a big juggernaut and once it was moving it was very difficult for me to get back in!

3.4.4 'On the road' management

One company highlighted the important management role of the stage manager, especially where touring productions were concerned. Very often this work involved managing the performers, and managing relations with the host organisation, often through teachers in schools. Clearly, familiarity with the venues and the individual contacts could have a significant effect on the smooth running of an event. While some companies were able to retain a permanent stage manager who could build up such knowledge, many could not, and they relied on a succession of freelance stage managers. At least one company expressed the desire to create a permanent post to address this. Another sought to create an education liaison post, part of which would involve taking on some aspects of project management.

3.5 The deliverers of education projects

The term 'mediator', rather than 'deliverer', has usually been preferred throughout this report. From the accounts given by interviewees, it seemed that the process of making an educational programme happen involved much more than the mere 'delivery' of a product, usually requiring the kind of interaction and creativity that might be expected of a teacher. (The term 'actor/teacher', once favoured in theatre in education companies, seems not to encompass the full range of functions involved in mounting education projects.)

3.5.1 The availability of core staff

During the 1970s and 1980s, many theatre companies had a long-term payroll of performers, as well as their staff of management, administrative and technical personnel. In many cases, this included a resident education section, often comprising a mixture of theatre-trained and education-trained workers. Due at least in part to financial considerations (but also for policy reasons), these ensembles gradually disappeared, to the point where there are now very few drama companies operating with a permanent performing team. Many do not retain a technical team, except the performance venue-based companies, and few include designers on their permanent staff. All have an artistic director (sometimes doubling in the role of chief executive) and some, though by no means all, have an education officer or community director. As has been described above, those personnel have a central role in the conception, design and management of education projects, but it would appear that the actual delivery is frequently in the hands of short-term freelance staff.

3.5.2 Freelance mediation

A number of different patterns of relating to freelance education project mediators has become apparent.

Core freelance mediation

Some projects were mediated by frequently used freelance artists. In one case, a project described involved an actor for whom it was his twentieth production with the company – he was apparently a permanent member in all but name, and contract.

Several companies made regular use of technical and design staff. One company was looking to create a permanent stage management post because of the importance of building up a familiarity with the venues and contacts encountered in touring to the same venues. Freelance education workshop leaders were also used repeatedly by some companies.

Contracting to other organisations

Two projects were described that involved the contracting of an entire arts company by the initiating company, delivering a range of skills or even another specialist artform skill. A company coordinator described how a dance company was engaged to deliver a project for which the theatre company was not equipped.

> *I suggested them and then they sent a representative along who agreed to do it and she was then involved in the planning of all the sessions as well;* [the dance company] *themselves contributed some of the money as well. I mean they contributed all the planning sessions, and then all the preliminary sessions were paid for by the project.*

Freelance teams

Many projects involved the bringing together of a one-off combination of artists, chosen for their unique range of skills, tailored to the precise needs of the project. This applied especially to the selection of actors, but also to the range of artform expertise needed for a participatory project. One such involved an actor, a dancer, a choreographer, two writers and a musician coming together for the same project.

3.5.3 Issues relating to the use of freelance workers to mediate projects

Continuity

A number of issues arose from this heavy reliance on freelance artists who did not have an ongoing relationship to the company. Some companies noted a need to either train or orient each new team of artists to the needs, context and style of the company in preparation for each new project. Where the same staff were used repeatedly, this could result in a valued familiarity between the deliverers and the audiences or participants. This applied to performers, stage managers and education workshop mediators.

Instability

From the point of view of some freelancers, there was instability and possibly greater financial hardship, one such person expressing great concern that she would be unable to continue with the development of a line of education work because of the need to obtain regular employment.

> *I mean, to be honest, I just cannot as it stands continue to do this kind of work because I'm reaching a point, you know ... I just cannot financially survive.*

It may well be that others preferred the freedom of freelance working. It may be that this type of employment pattern makes it less likely that the deliverers are able to receive training to update either their artistic or their educational skills, although 'on-the-job' training while preparing for projects was valued by some interviewees.

> [The director] *would entrust you to do whatever workshop it is or follow the way he does his workshop, which is in his own particular way. Training on the job really or by watching or by following him, and I think you know that tends to be the way it works.*

Flexibility or financial constraint

It would appear that the main reason for the prevalent use of freelancers for project mediation was financial, in that these workers needed only be paid for the periods of rehearsal/preparation and delivery, while most of the development work was undertaken by the small core staff. However, the method also gave the companies freedom to select those with the particular skills or characteristics needed for the project in hand. As has recently happened with some repertory theatres, some companies were considering ways to employ on a longer-term basis in order to enable a more developmental approach.

> *One other possibility that we've always thought about, although I think it would be very difficult, it would be a hell of a tough job, would be having an education team that was here permanently because as you've just been saying when you asked me about the weeks* [per year spent on education projects], *you could almost go from one job to another and it could almost be a group of five people's full-time job.*

Another director put such a desire clearly in the realm of development, both of the artists and the work itself.

> *The only way you can really learn how to do that work is by doing it, but I think they need more support around them while they are doing it, and I am hoping that's what an outlook director will bring to that situation and then what you ideally would like is actors who have had the experience of doing one tour, will then bring it into the next one, but it's very difficult.*

3.6 Project design features

3.6.1 Variations

As part of the research interviewing process, theatre company members in each case study were invited to describe in some detail one of the education projects that had recently been undertaken by their company. It was left to them to identify what qualified as an education project. The view that *all theatre is educational* was expressed by one interviewee; for some interviewees, *education is their core work*; and for others, *education is at the core* of their work. Therefore, in selecting the project to describe, interviewees, chose examples that others may not regard as education projects at all. Consequently, the range of design features is very wide. This is compounded by the range of companies themselves, in terms of size, location, purpose and aims, and their need to invent designs to suit their particular circumstances.

3.6.2 Design features

While there was very little commonality in the overall structure of projects delivered by different companies, all employed various combinations of the design features listed below. These are broad categories, each of them being realised with very different design details, intentions and characters.

Professional theatre performances

These took place in the company's own venue, or in community venues, often schools, youth clubs or other community facilities. Some were designed with specific audiences in mind, and others were for more general audiences. They may or may not be promoted to their audiences as educational events.

Packages accompanying professional performances

These included:

♦ Theatre Days or Play Days, presented in the theatre venue to explore aspects of the production and the process of theatre making in order to enhance the audience's experience of the play in question.

♦ Pre- or post-show discussions – in a sense a scaled down version of the previous category, but without the more practical elements.

Workshops in preparation for the performance that the participants are due to see later

These took place in the participants' usual place of education, though one company cited instances where schools could not accommodate such workshops, and they had to be delivered in the performance venue. Workshops, as the ubiquitous name suggests, involve activity by the participants.

Publications

These offered information and ideas about the production under examination, and were usually aimed at teachers, though some contained sections for the direct consumption of the learners.

Community productions

These included productions by youth theatre groups, alliances of school and other community groups, and any production where the target group were themselves the performers (and crew) rather than being the audience to a professional production. An often extended period of education and training in theatre skills culminated in a performance, often to the public, sometimes as paying customers, in the theatre's main venue or in the community, even as an outdoor perambulatory performance in one case.

Summer schools

These shared some of the same characteristics as the previous model, but the balance tended to be tilted more towards the process, involving an intensive period of theatre making which may lead to a performance, but perhaps with a lower public profile.

Youth theatre training projects

These were related to the previous model, but this time structured as a pre-professional training experience, extending over a period of months or years, and possibly concluding in a public presentation.

Arts management training course

This model offered a pre-professional training experience in short course form to those intending to enter a career in theatre administration or management.

Ongoing professional theatre staff support for local projects

Company members worked with groups such as youth theatres, in one example extending to the development, establishment and ongoing support for an international pairing of youth arts groups.

The management and promotion of the delivery of courses or projects in other artforms

One such example was a dance group working with patients in a fracture clinic on a weekly basis.

This is certainly not an exhaustive list of design features, and arts organisations will constantly devise new ones. These are ones identified from our interviews, and they were often combined in individual education projects, and used by different companies for different purposes.

3.7 Blueprints, development, diversity and flexibility

3.7.1 Reasons for variety

As stated earlier, there was little commonality between the case study companies as far as their 'product design' was concerned. Given the varying nature of the companies, their sizes, geographical circumstances, funding remit and inherent purposes, this was not surprising. New writing, international promotion, rural communities, the youth sector, regional mainstream, children's theatre and ethnically specific work all require different approaches. So while most companies used several of the design features listed above, the eventual designs showed little similarity, and what is more, there was some evidence to suggest that there was little awareness between companies of what models were being used. Some freelance workers in particular lamented the lack of opportunity to discover more about what was being offered elsewhere. This may be due to an absence of forums in which such learning can take place, or to a lack of access by freelance workers to such forums as do exist.

3.7.2 Use of blueprints

While different companies appeared not to be operating to the same blueprints, some companies clearly repeated certain structures, and applied them to changing contents. For one company, this comprised the majority of their education work, which in turn was a sizeable proportion of their entire output. They used a model that had served them well for a number of years, and each year a different text was addressed by that model. Their most recent manifestation underwent significant structural changes, but the overall method remained intact.

> *I put to [the director] last year a possible refinement of that. I said that first of all, for one reason or another, we were running out of our pool of people and that secondly other projects that I'd done for my own company involved the actors in running the workshops, the same actors who are in the show, and that had a number of educational advantages.*

It is likely that the familiarity of teachers with the model generated confidence in the product, and this would be borne out by the fact that some teachers chose to extend the participant age range, as a result of which some reception classes had an experience of Shakespeare in performance.

3.7.3 Blueprints with variations

Another company seemed to apply essentially the same workshop structure to different productions of new and contemporary writing. However, within the overall format, the director was at pains to respond to individual requests from teachers to adjust the sessions to suit particular aspects of the production under consideration, or particular lines of study that the students were engaged in at that time, such as text work.

In another case, the company regularly offered Theatre Days, which contained a number of frequently used ingredients. However, where the play offered opportunities for the involvement of a local museum, the format accommodated its contribution.

One theatre's regular commitment to an annual Youth Theatre Summer School, in 2000 deviated from the normal production of an existing text.

This year the director wanted to devise around story-telling [his area of interest]. *Interestingly, the young people were not interested in the stories he had chosen, so they ended up using bits of his influences, but much more from the young people themselves. It meant everyone had to do more work, but it was great!*

3.7.4 The need to innovate

Project descriptions by interviewees clearly indicated an excitement with what was new. Breaking new ground is what most artists aspire to do. Since this research project has not addressed the perceptions of teachers or client groups, it is not known to what extent they are also committed to novelty, or to what extent they value having some familiarity at least with the form of the experiences to which they subscribe. Some interviewees referred to the intention to inspire and excite, suggesting that they also believed that the capacity to surprise was part of their stock in trade. Certainly, of the examples described by interviewees, many were perceived as being major departures from their previous work, involving new research and development, and many were cited as being in response to changing contextual factors, including changing funding opportunities, external requests for particular work, curriculum opportunities or the Millennium.

3.7.5 Development and progression

The extent to which companies offered a strategic, developmental progression in their work was not clear. Some education projects took a long-term view, for example in developing potential future performers, or penetrating new touring areas to be further developed in the future, but projects were also conceived as creative ideas, or in response to external requests. Most projects sat very clearly in the client-centred educational aims of the company, although some interviewees expressed concern that they were expected to deliver too wide a range of services, and found it difficult to turn down requests. But the extent to which their consistent dedication to their own aims produced a sense of development for the clients was uncertain. One company pointed out that the schoolchildren in their area were likely to have four experiences of a professional Shakespeare production during their school life, graduating from primary Shakespeare projects to secondary ones. Another director valued the familiarity built up between himself, as a workshop leader, and the teachers to whom he often returned, believing that this generated a better use of the experiences. One freelance actor working regularly with a company touring plays to community venues felt that his repeated visits to the same venues enhanced the experience both for himself and for the audiences.

However, none of the above examples gave a clear sense of development of the material as experienced by audience members year on year, other than one director believing that they got it better each time, partly because of evaluation. There were examples of projects developing from previous ones, in response to client demand, and these amounted to examples of developmental approaches. One project with an intended lifespan of three years was expected to have a developmental impact on the participants.

This raises the question of the responsibility of theatre companies to the educational development of their clients. It can be argued that that is the responsibility of the teachers, to assemble a range of artistic inputs, from a variety of sources that serve the needs of their students. Whether theatre companies individually or in collaboration with other arts organisations can facilitate such a strategic approach by teachers might be worth investigating. Some interviewees have indicated that the 'outsider' role of the artist is an important feature of their contribution to education.

3.8   Participating groups and clients

3.8.1 Schools and communities

Although a very significant proportion of work was generated specifically for schools, much work was not. Indeed, several companies had no hesitation in including what some might classify as community theatre in their education portfolios. They drew no distinction between educational aims and community development aims.

> *We don't see education as sitting down and teaching people; we see it as providing people with experiences and opportunities for involvement and for expression, and I think that is done in different ways but to the same extent in terms of touring theatre communities and getting those communities involved in participatory art.*

More than one interviewee expressed reservations about either the commitment or capacity of schools to utilise theatre services. In one case, the company had previously had little relationship with schools, but was now starting to work with them as a gateway to the community, and expected this to become a significant feature of their work. Another company bemoaned the lack of support from their most local schools, in contrast to a third which felt it had very strong local school connections and support.

3.8.2 Age ranges and intergenerational education

When lifelong learning opportunities in a small rural community were addressed, intergenerational understanding was both a community and an educational issue. Similarly, in an urban setting, what started as a primary school project evolved very naturally into a community project with senior citizens and other community groups building on the experience and expertise of the original young participants. The intergenerational component emerged in a very different form for a company offering Theatre Days, since these were open to the general public as well as school groups, and tended to attract retired people in considerable numbers, occurring as they invariably did during normal working days.

Older people were also the main participants in a project sponsored by a hospital fracture clinic. The artform in that case happened to be dance, but had been set up by a theatre company as part of its expanding participatory arts regional remit. At the other end of the age range, teachers themselves extended the audience age group to include children as young as four in a project designed for six to 11 only. Otherwise there seemed to be a fairly even spread of projects across the school age range, even though the relative inflexibility of secondary schools to accommodate incoming events was referred to more than once.

3.8.3 Teachers as learners

Several companies referred to activities aimed at teachers as learners. For example, one company referred to workshops on theatre design for teachers, and another regarded its teachers' forum as having an educational as well as a consultative function. There was no mention from any interviewees of teachers being *indirectly* targeted through their pupils, although the nature of many projects would suggest that teachers may well have experienced some kind of professional development. This is not to suggest that teachers' needs were being ignored. Many projects were designed with the conscious intention to deliver educational objectives required by teachers for their pupils, and many projects involved the creation of support materials for use by teachers.

It may well be that the potential for companies to support the professional development of teachers could be exploited more fully without substantially disturbing the nature of the product on offer.

Young people

Quite apart from the school sector, much work was undertaken with young people, either as members of an existing youth group (youth club or youth theatre) or as a new configuration of young people brought together for the purposes of the project. In one case, a youth theatre group and an adult community theatre were brought together to create a new production.

3.8.4 Audience development as an educational aim

It was clear that all of the case study companies worked with their client groups in order to give them a quality experience within the project itself. Obviously, where a preparatory workshop prior to a performance was concerned, the intention was to enhance the experience of that performance. It was equally clear that many companies were very conscious of the potential impact on theatre attendance in the future. One company was very concerned that its audience base was relatively narrow, but was very committed to the view that a wider cross-section of the population would appreciate the work they were promoting, if only they felt they had access to it. Another was delighted to discover that their community production had resulted in a 28 per cent first time attendance bonus, and was seeking ways to retain that new body of theatregoers. Yet another company was committed to making theatre attendance a possibility for communities for whom geographic and demographic factors made theatre attendance very difficult. One company had evidence that their work in local primary schools resulted in some additional attendance at the theatre by other family members.

These examples would lead one to suggest that educational experiences and audience development covered a great deal of similar ground, and an appreciated educational experience could lead to greater uptake of 'non-educational' theatre opportunities without in any way compromising the educational intention. While some interviewees expressed concern that they were tending to work repeatedly with the same clients, all were clearly committed to finding ways to extend participation in their educational activities, as evidenced in the examples they described.

3.9   Community involvement in education work

3.9.1 Meanings of 'community'

The research sought to ascertain the relationship of theatre companies to their local communities. 'Local' can mean different things in different places. In a town of ten million people, local might mean within one mile. In a low population rural area, local could extend over several miles. The range of purposes for the ten case studies in this research inevitably meant vast variation in the ways that companies related to their communities, and in some cases there was simply no comparison between examples.

A touring company whose sole function was the national touring of new and challenging contemporary plays, and who were based in ex-commercial business offices, had no relationship to their local community. As far as education was concerned, they had a loyal, demanding and scattered clientele of schools and colleges around the country, and in a recent tour of workshops supporting a production, used their familiarity with those schools to refine and adapt their product.

One regional theatre company characterised itself as being the only building-based theatre company for many miles. It consequently related to a population travelling considerable distances, both as audience and as participants in community and educational activities. It also related more intimately to the community of its own very local neighbourhood, through having recently mounted a production about a neighbouring street.

3.9.2 The nature of community relationships

A 'suburban' repertory theatre described a range of contacts with its local community, both through its workshop and performance work with local schools, and through involvement in the local arts forum. However, another suburban-based organisation, providing a specialist product for a much wider constituency, referred to very poor relations with its local schools.

A metropolitan organisation with a national and international clientele had been seeking to deepen its community accessibility by working with local community configurations, and described a project, based in a different part of the metropolis, that brought together international artists with local people.

> *I am very passionately interested in what people call the cross-over ... I want people to go and see other things in* [the festival] *because I think they're fantastic. I want them to feel that they can travel across the city to see things because they're motivated to do so and they're not locked in their own little localities because they don't think there's anything else out there for them.*

A company with a rural remit chose for one of its latest productions to base its rehearsal period in a small rural community, rather than at its own more than adequate base, so that the experience of working within that community would inform the content of the play itself.

Several companies described ongoing projects for local young people, working either in youth clubs or coming together for specialist theatre courses.

From the examples above, it would be very difficult to classify overall relationships with communities, the contextual factors being so varied. The location of work, be it in a company's home base or venue, or in a community setting, would seem to have little bearing on the extent or significance of community involvement, though a national touring remit is an exception. The fundamental purpose of the company would seem to be the only significant factor in most cases.

3.10 Partnerships in education projects

Partnership has become one of the great buzzwords in both the arts and education sectors, and we attempt below to categorise the variety of examples of partnership apparent in the examples cited by interviewees. We have divided them initially into funding relationships and working relationships.

3.10.1 Funding partnerships

In a very broad sense of the word, the funding relationship can be called a partnership, in which both the funder and the arts organisation share the same objectives, one of them contributing the finance and the other the labour. In some cases, a more active participation on the part of the funders was described:

> *We did apply for the whole three years, but* [the Regional Arts Board] *have given us what we asked for, for year one, so depending on the success or otherwise – according to* [the Regional Arts Board] *– how year one goes will depend on how successful we are, I would imagine, in obtaining funding for years two and three.*

In other instances, the relationship seemed to be much closer to that of purchaser and provider. For example, an annual grant was received to tour to schools in a specific area, but little evidence of involvement beyond that was apparent.

Projects described involved the following funding arrangements.

Projects funded out of the organisation's core funding

Core funding for all companies was from the arts funding system (ACE or RAB) or the local authority. In the former case, funding for education was never earmarked, and it was at the discretion of the company management how much was allocated to education projects. This varied enormously, depending on the nature and purposes of the company. In one case, almost a quarter of a million pounds was allocated to a single education project. Another education project was conducted with a small amount of hidden subsidy in the form of company administrative support. Local authority support, if delivered through the education department, was always provided specifically for the education programme. In one case, this enabled a company to geographically extend its touring area with a schools project. One company pointed out that its core local authority funding (not delivered via the education department) came with the tacit understanding that education work would be delivered; indeed, when the company had to temporarily close for financial reasons, the education project continued in order to ensure the continued support of the local authority on the resumption of normal services. (This is in marked contrast to a situation some years ago when a company, in similar financial difficulties, closed its successful education section in order to ensure the survival of its main house operation.)

Projects attracting specific financial support

In the examples given, these came from a wide variety of sources.

♦ Project grants from arts funding sources, meeting a particular, sometimes temporary, priority of the funder, and beyond the expectations of the core grant. One example was an RAB providing additional support for a tour of a rural area that had recently become part of its geographical remit.

♦ Regional Arts Lottery Programme (RALP) funding contributed to some projects, in one case seeding a new programme of workshops, since which time further developments of the project had to proceed without additional grant aid.

- Millennium Lottery Board funding enabled the initial working on one project, and this led to an unpredicted large investment from the company's core funding. Another project was funded from this source, but indirectly through another organisation.

- Local authority departments contributed to projects, as did health authorities and fire services. (In kind support, from staff from such bodies being involved in planning or recruitment should not be overlooked.)

- One project received financial support from an Education Action Zone.

- We were not able to identify any commercial sponsorship for the projects under consideration, but this may be the result of incomplete data.

The need to attract extra funding

Several interviewees made it clear that a large proportion of their education work could only take place through the attraction of additional project funding. Although some regarded themselves as very accomplished in accessing such funds, they also resented the time needed to generate applications, often for sums that hardly merited the effort, and which were inevitably short term.

> *It is very easy ... you know the sector ... all those schemes that have been kind of run up the flag pole and suddenly everybody's chasing that really, redirecting or redescribing what you do to get an extra bit of cash ... I mean the amount of energy and effort put into that isn't worth the return.*

(One company volunteered that they found it easier to access project funding for their education work than raise funds for their 'core' artistic activity, and were fearful that if the latter suffered too much from lack of funding, the education work inspired by it would suffer greatly.)

3.10.2 Working partnerships

The concept of partnership, which for some time has been given a great deal of encouragement in the arts world, is now receiving some critical evaluation. As one manager pointed out:

> *The thing about partnerships can mean 'we've got this, you've got that', together you get the lowest common denominator out of the two, you know.*

This perhaps rather grim observation may be accurate on occasions, but there appeared to have been some very well-regarded examples of partnership working as well.

What for some has come to be called partnership working may in fact be little more than a mediated consumer/provider relationship, with the consumer (or sponsor) having some influence on the product design prior to delivery, as is the case in many commercial transactions. The degree and nature of partnership working varied greatly.

Partnerships between arts organisations

In one case, three theatre companies collaborated on a piece of theatre that then became a tour in each of their areas. Although initiated by one company, the funding, staffing and management were shared, although the creative process was initially located with the initiating company. Another form of partnership involved the initiating company contracting a second arts organisation to deliver the project, under the management of the first company. A third project involved the initiating company devising the process with another theatre organisation, this one a venue, using the contacts and expertise of a third company, and then the three of them contracting freelance workers to mediate the project. Not all companies generated partnerships of this kind, but those that did seemed to do so repeatedly. Size appeared not to be the deciding factor.

Partnerships with other cultural institutions

Two companies cited examples of projects in which museums were partners in either the development or the delivery of projects.

Partnerships with other bodies

Examples were cited in which theatre companies worked with fire services and health departments. In both cases, the relationship went beyond that of purchaser/provider, and involved advice and guidance on the nature of the work.

Partnerships with the education sector

In describing certain projects, interviewees included local education advisers and teachers amongst the partners or collaborators, rather than simply describing them as clients. However, the general impression was that education advisory staff did not usually become closely involved, retaining a rather distant advisory function, whereas in some case teachers were a minor but significant part of the mediation of projects.

Partnerships with the community

This seemed to take a wide variety of forms, and the distinction between the community as partners and as participants was very blurred. A frequent community function was the recruitment of project participants, and community members were often involved in organising venues, and in one case events or activities peripheral to the drama experience.

> So at its simplest, it could be, you know, ... a talk out from the actors, but I'm more interested in maybe a meal, maybe fireworks, maybe a speaker from the rural regeneration ... you know ... so that you can offer a number of options to a community and say 'theatre isn't just about sitting for two hours with an interval in the middle'.

3.11 Examples of projects and how they relate to educational aims

3.11.1 Approach to the section

Chapter 2 proposed a typology of educational aims as described by the case study theatre companies. It described a continuum of aims, ranging from those that are totally integrated within the company's artistic mission, to educational aims that deliver the needs of the theatre company itself. Arguably, all of the case study companies professed aims that fit into each of the five categories, but in describing recent sample projects, it is clear that not all aims are delivered through every project.

In this section, we briefly describe ten examples of education projects as identified and selected by the interviewees. They ranged from highly resourced, large-scale performance pieces to small, almost cost-free workshops in school classrooms. All of the projects appeared to deliver more than one of the categories of aims described earlier. Each one of those categories appeared to take primacy in at least one of the projects described, except for the last one – aims relating to the needs of the theatre company (though these appeared as subsidiary aims in virtually every example cited.)

The broad categories of educational aims are as follows:

- **A. Educational aims which are totally integrated with artistic aims**
- **B. Drama or theatre-centred educational aims**
- **C. Curriculum development and support aims**
- **D. Client-centred educational aims**
- **E. Aims relating to the needs of the theatre company.**

Throughout this chapter, specific aims and objectives are cross-referenced (in brackets) to the typology in Chapter 2, where further information can be found. To provide a rational order for describing the examples offered by interviewees, we have chosen to describe each project under the aims category that appears to us to be particularly important for that project. However, it may not be the *most* important aims category, either in our minds or those of the company members, and we also attempt to describe how the full range of aims is being addressed by each project.

It was not the remit of this research to assess the extent to which aims were being delivered by the companies. The following analysis simply attempts to ascertain which educational aims were *addressed* by each project example, and therefore indicates the extent to which aims *could* be delivered.

3.11.2 The examples

Educational aims which are totally integrated with artistic aims

Example 1

> A company with a rural remit decided to create a touring theatre piece aimed particularly at communities generally regarded as too small to support a touring production. They wanted a piece that would appeal to the whole community, and that would stimulate intergenerational dialogue. They chose to locate the rehearsal period not in their own base, but in a small village that was part of an area that had recently been added to their touring remit. The play that resulted involved a grandfather and granddaughter, looking at their relationship with each other, with place and with the continuity, and discontinuity, of their lives. The production played in village venues, usually school halls, at times that would best suit the local community – sometimes at the start of the school day, and sometimes at twilight, thus increasing the chances of attracting a mixed audience, usually of teachers, children, their parents and grandparents. Each performance was followed by informal discussion, frequently involving individuals from across that range.

The company regarded this project as educational in the same way that the rest of its product was educational. With general aims that focused on 'rural' and 'community' as central to their purpose, the play and discussion directly addressed one of their priorities, intergenerational communication. Both the play and the discussion following it enabled the audience to consider more deeply how generations relate to each other, how changes such as death affect those left behind.

♦ In that sense, educational aims totally integrated with artistic aims (A) are the basis of the production.

♦ The project appeared not to address any *drama/theatre-centred education aims* (B).

♦ Although usually performed in school venues, there was no evidence to suggest that the play was intended to be used as a *resource for curriculum development* or support, though it is hard to imagine that an event of this nature never generated discussion or other school work after the event (C).

♦ However, client-centred educational aims (D) were clearly to the fore, both in terms of *personal development* and *in relation to the community* (D7 and D8). Though the content could well have been equally appropriate to any other community, the organisation of the event was clearly in *response to geographical needs* (D9).

♦ Although not explicitly so, the project appeared to *deliver aims relating to the survival of the company* (E11) – it had recently been given additional funding to serve a particular geographical area and needed to demonstrate that it was doing so. *Audience development* (especially under E11ai), was in fact a primary impetus for the project, not for the benefit of the company, but because broadening access to theatre performances, especially in rural areas, was the *raison d'être* of the company.

Drama/theatre-centred educational aims

Example 2

A theatre ran a regular three-week summer school for young people, fulfilling the remit of its local education authority funding. A group of 15+ students worked with a professional director and technical staff to create a production, working as closely as possible to a professional process. On this occasion, the director chose not to use an existing script, but to devise a performance using storytelling techniques. The students preferred to use their own ideas rather than those offered by the director, and although this generated extra work, this was welcomed. The project culminated in a public performance, getting as close to professional standards as possible, with the workers enabling the young people's efforts. Apart from the lighting designer, staff were freelance contracted workers, and other than using the theatre's stage and rehearsal space, there was little connection with the core activity of the theatre. Participants paid a fee to take part, and the remainder of the cost was met from the theatre's overall budget.

- ◆ This approach, not unique to this company, was largely driven by the aim to *develop practical theatre skills* (B1). Its concentration on professional theatre practices and standards seemed to take precedence over other possible aims.

- ◆ However, one might assume that some client-centred educational aims, especially those relating to *personal development* (D7) would have been delivered, especially D7a, c and d.

- ◆ By working with *young people outside of the school setting*, it also served aim 8c.

- ◆ Although not mentioned by any interviewees, the experience could well have had an effect on *audience development* (E11a), and in that the project was an outcome expected from local authority funding, it delivered aim E11b *to attract funding.*

Example 3

A theatre company ran regular Theatre Days, based on productions in its main repertoire, aimed at giving the public an insight into the making of the production, *'to turn a production inside out'*. The origin of the approach went back some way, and was by no means confined to this theatre. Here, the event was sometimes organised in conjunction with the local museum, which might focus on social history and costume where the production was a period drama. The day would concentrate on one particular focus, such as set design, costume, or new technology, depending on the particular elements of the production under consideration. Its structure would be generated by the play's director, in conjunction with the education officer, bringing in the museum staff and particular technical specialists as appropriate. The actors would also be involved, often taking part in a simulated scene rehearsal. Audiences tended to be made up of a combination of school groups and individuals, many of whom were older people. The cost of such an exercise to the theatre was relatively low, since the personnel were undertaking the work in their normally contracted time, and the theatre space was already set up for the event. However, some staff were reluctant to contribute to sections of the event themselves, simply because of lack of experience and/or confidence, which the theatre found difficult to overcome with training.

- This project most directly addressed the aim '*to develop the capacity for critical appreciation of theatre*' (B2). From the description of the various elements that went to make up the event, all three of the sub-aims were addressed, with the involvement of the local museum giving additional weight to the aim to extend the *knowledge of the historical context* of plays and writers.

- Given that audiences tended to be largely made up of school parties, some *curriculum aims* (C) were met, especially in supporting teachers in *their teaching of theatre studies*. Since other audience members were frequently of retirement age, *supporting lifelong learning* (D8aiii) was covered.

- Using this approach gave the general public, students or otherwise, a greater understanding not only of the play under consideration, but also of the nature and working of theatre. As such it had an *audience development* function, giving more people access to a meaningful experience of theatre (E11a).

Curriculum development and support

Example 4

A small building-based company annually produced a series of productions of Shakespeare plays for schools. The most recent primary school project involved changes to the format that had been used over recent years. Previously, education specialists would visit participating schools to run workshops on the play prior to the start of its performance run. This time, the actors themselves visited schools during the first part of each week to run the workshops, so that the pupils would then see the same people on stage in performance at the end of the week, and be involved in minor audience participation as well. Generating a confidence with the use of Shakespeare's language was regarded as a priority aim. The original format for the workshops had been devised by a previous trainee director and his wife who at the time had been studying methods for teaching Shakespeare, and they continued to devise the workshop content each year. Having originally started as a project for six- to 11-year-olds, some schools chose to also involve pupils from their reception classes. Workshops happened in each school, and the pupils then visited the theatre for the performance itself. Directors and actors were contracted freelance artists, and the project was managed by the theatre's team of administrators. Some of the theatre's financial subsidy was earmarked specifically for school work, but most of the costs were covered by the theatre's general budget and fees from schools. The theatre was aware that for the local authority, the work for schools partly justified its grant to the theatre as a whole.

With the study of Shakespeare now featuring in the National Curriculum at key stage 2, some theatre companies are delivering support for what many teachers have seen as a very difficult task. The appetite for such a service would appear to be substantial, with teachers themselves extending the age range of pupils exposed to this work.

- This project supported the primary *history* curriculum (C4b), but, once again, although teachers may well be learning themselves from the experience, that appeared not to be part of the company's aims (C3).

The combination of the workshop with the performance in the theatre suggested a fairly self-contained learning package, more specific than simply providing *a theatrical performance as a resource for schools* (C5).

♦ It appeared that the aims under B2, *to develop a capacity for critical appreciation of theatre*, were addressed here, especially in informing the learners about a particular piece (B2b).

♦ The participatory approach of the workshop, and the limited participation in the performance that it led to, indicated that client-centred educational aims *concerning self-expression and social interaction* were addressed (D7c and d).

♦ Although those responsible for the design and delivery of the project were concerned only with the education and development of the students, management expressed an awareness of the potential for the pupils' experience to increase the chances of their parents and family using the theatre in the future. *Audience development* aims (11a), in the sense of increasing future audiences, may thus have been achieved directly, with the students, and as a word-of-mouth awareness-raising for the theatre.

♦ The delivery of a service for local schools was also seen as essential in order that the local authority could justify its investment in the theatre as a whole (E11b). (This was another example of companies finding it easier *to attract funding* for educational activities than to support their core artistic activities.)

Example 5

A theatre company that was funded to produce only children's theatre responded to requests from schoolteachers to present a Shakespeare play. Following consultation with their teachers' advisory panel, they decided on *The Tempest*. As well as presenting the play itself as a professional production, the company invited six middle schools in its local area to create their own performances based on the themes in the play. On each of three days, two schools would come into the theatre, spend the morning in technical preparation, and show the performance to its own pupils and staff, as well as to the other school participating on that day. The theatre provided stage management, technical staff, front of house support and the guidance of its education officer. Using the theatre at a time when it would otherwise have been 'dark', and grant support from the Shakespeare Millennium Trust, meant that the project was financially viable. The pupils were then encouraged to attend the company's production of *The Tempest*, but under their own steam rather than in school parties.

♦ This was one of few examples where a project had been created explicitly in response to client demand. In that respect, it fulfilled aim D9a, *responding to school needs*.

♦ The company, by organising and supporting productions in a number of schools, was meeting a number of aims, including *supporting teachers in their teaching* (C4) and, intentionally or otherwise, *raising the profile of drama in schools* (C6). (Although this particular project did not contain any component aimed directly at supporting teacher education and training, this was one of the few case study companies that did offer such projects.)

♦ The school production element of the project also addressed certain client-centred educational aims, especially those concerned *with personal development through self-expression* (D7c).

♦ The fact that the pupils' productions were mounted in the theatre directly developed *their practical theatre skills* in a way otherwise unavailable to teachers (B1).

♦ The school pupils were encouraged to attend the company's production of *The Tempest*, not as school parties but as individuals, the assumption being that their parents would attend with them. This was thus an *audience development* strategy, aimed at securing the survival of the company (E11a).

Example 6

A national middle-scale touring company revived a much acclaimed play from the 1980s. This was done largely because of the quality of the play, but was timely in that in the intervening years it had also achieved the status of an A-level set text. The director responded to the requests of teachers in schools and FE colleges to provide workshops about the play. These were about both theatre as an art form, and about the historical context of the play. Their purpose was to enrich the audience's understanding and appreciation of the play. They employed techniques that the director had used while directing the production, and would be adapted to suit the particular requirements of the teacher, if appropriate (e.g. more accent on text etc.). The director devised the workshop, and trained an assistant director, working with some of the actors, to present their own version of his format, although he continued to run a considerable proportion of workshops himself. Workshops on this particular production continued to be made available even after the end of the tour, in response to demand from teachers. (Workshops of a similar nature have been offered with all subsequent productions.) The programme of workshops was self-financing, through fees from schools and colleges, although a small grant had been received to produce the accompanying teacher's pack, the production of which was assisted by the education officer of a specialist museum.

♦ Like the previous example, the company responded to teacher requests in devising this programme of workshops, and not surprisingly the main aim *was curriculum development and support* (C4). In this case, the curriculum support element was very specific, and was the only example where examination coursework was directly addressed.

♦ However, this was also a manifestation of the wider educational aim of a company dedicated to making challenging contemporary theatre more accessible to a wider audience, and as such delivered *drama and theatre-centred educational aims*, in particular to *develop the capacity for critical appreciation of theatre* (B2).

♦ In developing the skills of company members, the project *provided creative opportunities for theatre artists* (E10b), and had a clear *audience development* remit, in that it sought to make difficult dramatic material more accessible to a wider audience (E11a).

♦ Given the radical nature of the company's selected plays, it could also be said that such workshops address the aim *to open alternative perspectives/challenges to the status quo* (D7bii).

Client-centred educational aims

Although the examples described under this heading were not targeted at schools, many of the aims of category D were addressed in schools, as can be seen in the analysis of the aims of other examples.

Example 7

A large regional repertory theatre decided to mount a major project to mark the Millennium, but did not want to deal with the kind of 'heritage' subject that might be expected of it in such circumstances. Instead, it chose to explore the life of its adjacent street, a location famous and infamous in the town for its variety of life. Initially planned by the chief executive and an associate artistic director, the project eventually involved the entire theatre staff, and culminated in a two-week performance run on the company's main stage, involving about 280 of the local population. The management of the project was handed to a freelance project manager who worked on the piece for about 18 months. Local community groups, the theatre's youth theatre and community theatre groups, schools and the local press were all involved in the recruitment of the performing company, for which over 1,000 people applied. The performance played to capacity audiences, and attracted about 28 per cent of new theatre attenders.

♦ All of the *aims relating to personal development* (D7a–d) were addressed in this project, partly through the process undertaken by the participants, but also through the nature of the content of the piece.

♦ *Aims relating to the community* (D8a–c) seemed to be central to the nature of the project. Social issues of *cultural diversity, social inclusion and lifelong learning* were all addressed in relation to a specific geographic location, *and young people out of school* were high on the participant target list.

♦ Although these client-centred educational aims seemed to be central to the project, several other aims also came into play. By making the production part of the main stage programme, the educational aims became *totally integrated with artistic aims* (A).

♦ By allocating virtually the entire creative and technical staff to the project, the *practical theatre skills* of participants were developed (B1).

♦ Aims relating to the needs of theatre companies were delivered, especially in that it provided *creative opportunities for theatre artists* (E10b), it involved the *commissioning of both new writing and new music* (E10c) and had an impressive effect on *audience development* (E11a). Although the project did attract additional *funding* (E11b), it is certainly true that the draw on the theatre's core artistic budget was vastly (and perhaps unpredictably) greater than the additional income.

As the company itself pointed out, this project was very much a one-off, and is unlikely to be repeated for some time, despite its palpable success. However, capitalising on that success is seen as a priority by the company.

Example 8

> Having created a very successful performance event to celebrate the fiftieth anniversary of the arrival of the SS Windrush from the Caribbean, a company with the remit to work with the Black community set up a performance festival 18 months later.
>
> The core of the event was three commissioned music theatre pieces, each 15 minutes long. Alongside these, were a range of activities, including an art installation, a multi-media event and three debates about the arts in the context of Black people's experience. The target group was the 16 to 35 age range, a majority of whom were from ethnic minorities, and most of the ticket purchases were by women. The venue was a local community centre attached to a chapel, and the event was unexpectedly successful in terms of attendances, having to turn away a large number of people.

This project might equally have located under category A aims, in which educational aims are totally integrated with artistic aims, this event being part of the core activity of the company.

♦ *Aims relating to the community* were most important to the project (D8), with the issue of *social inclusion* high on the agenda. Although debates on the arts were part of the event, these did not appear to be directly concerned with developing a deeper understanding and appreciation of theatre form, more about exploring the cultural context and issues. In that respect, the aim *to offer alternative perspective/ challenge the status quo* (D7b) was addressed.

♦ One would need to extend the aim *towards the survival of theatre companies* (E11a) to include the arts in general in this case, and with particular reference to Black people, this being a fundamental aim of the company as a whole. Both the profile of the event, and its contents, suggested that this was thoroughly addressed.

♦ *Creative opportunities for Black artists* and the *commissioning of new writing and new music* (E10b and c) were all part of the package.

Example 9

Having commissioned a performance art company to work with a group of primary school children in a local community, the commissioning company was asked by that community what was going to happen next. Seeking to extend the range of people that the company normally related to, they decided to use the primary school experience as a gateway to wider community development, with a particular accent on intergenerational collaboration. Additional arts funding and Education Action Zone funding enabled the recruitment of freelance artists to lead a series of workshops that could develop the experience already gained by the children, but also attract the involvement of their parents, and indeed a group of older women from a local centre. These workshops led to the creation and performance of a perambulatory piece around the area where the project was located. At the time of the research, this phase of the project was being evaluated in order to clarify the direction that the next stage of the work would follow.

♦ This project evolved from a previous one, partly because of the demands of those that had been exposed to the first project, *responding to the needs of a specific geographical community* (D8b and 9c) which was itself responding to the stimulus offered by the company in the first place. Whereas the first project had centred more on school needs, this one focused on the community, but using the school experience as a community resource.

♦ *Opportunities for personal enrichment and enjoyment, self-expression and social interaction* were created (D7a, c and d), with an emphasis on intergenerational dialogue.

♦ Undertaking the work involved the development of *practical theatre skills* (B1).

♦ These were delivered by the generation *of creative opportunities for theatre* [and other] *artists* (E10b).

♦ One of the priorities for this particular company was to extend its activities more evenly over its two-year production cycle which revolved around a biennial festival, and to extend its clientele beyond the festival-goers by developing greater community links. Like much of its education programme, this project emerged from a festival event, and as such was conceived partly as an *audience development* project (E11a), having in part been developed by the marketing director.

Aims relating to the needs of theatre companies

Example 10

> A company that specialised in touring nationally to youth club venues undertook a long-term project to develop the theatre skills of Asian young people in their region. The original manifestation of the project in 1997 was intended to address the fact that there was a dearth of young, trained actors from the South Asian community available for casting. The later project, starting in the same location, but adding a second and a third location over the subsequent two years, was intended to culminate in a shared performance/celebration, with clear community development aims in addition to the original aims. The project was a collaboration between the touring company, a nearby small-scale theatre venue where the initial week-long course took place, and a local authority-run studio theatre. Performance (in drama, dance and music) rather than technical skills were prioritised, and were delivered by a carefully balanced selection of artists with different specialisms. The first part of the project was funded by the Regional Arts Board, and this was to be reviewed as progress was monitored. The project complemented the company's normal audience-based activities, targeted at a similar age group.

♦ Although the initial impetus for this project was to support the needs of the company, by *contributing to the development of the art of theatre* (E10a), the impact on the target group was probably more important to the company. It was an extension of one of the company's highest priorities, to serve the needs of the young Asian community, and in this case the needs of company and community met.

♦ Thus *the development of practical theatre skills* (B1) was clearly the central objective throughout the project.

♦ In delivering that aim, participants were given *opportunities for self-expression* (D7c), and the *opportunities for social interaction* (D7d) were intended to become increasingly important as the project extended to young people in different geographical communities. Given the target group, issues of cultural diversity were also important (D8ai).

Note

Although all of the examples above did in fact address a large number of the aims identified in Chapter 2, there is no virtue implied in covering many aims – sometimes there is a tight focus, and sometimes a broader sweep.

Because of the great variations in the nature and purposes of the companies studied, there was no clearly discernible pattern or prevalence of aims being addressed. While companies might possibly not feel that it was a priority, it was notable that aims relating to the needs of theatre companies (E) were being addressed in every project, deliberately or otherwise. It may be surprising that aims relating to curriculum development and support (C) were absent in half of the examples, and this would appear to be an indication of the scope of work defined by the companies as 'education'. It may also indicate some resistance to being used as a curriculum tool. In any case, interviewees tended to describe the distinctive contributions of theatre to education more in general educational terms than in curriculum terms, and consequently, category D aims were easily the most prevalent.

Whether or not all of the aims addressed consciously informed the planning process is not apparent from the research. The creative process usually started with the idea, rather than being a deliberate attempt to deliver one (or more) specific aim. That creative process happened within the context of the overall aims and ethos of the company, but cannot, and probably should not, be confined by a utilitarian delivery of predetermined agendas. Even by the end of a project, the mediators may not have been conscious of the extent to which some aims had been delivered (such as the effect on teacher professional development), and this in no way diminishes the value or effectiveness of that project.

However, by becoming more conscious of the extent to which they address educational aims, there may be a greater possibility of exploiting those educational possibilities more fully, without compromising the company's artistic aims and autonomy.

3.12 Evaluation and education projects

Rather like 'partnership', evaluation has been a regular talking point in the arts and education for some time. Nobody admitted to not doing evaluation, or to not valuing it, but the variety of purposes quoted, the variation in understanding of methods, and, most especially, the discrepancies concerning the impact of evaluation might cause one to question the extent of the commitment to evaluation.

3.12.1 Purposes of evaluation

The stated purposes for undertaking evaluation of projects fell loosely into three categories.

The development of future work by the company

There were several variations on this particular purpose. Several interviewees spoke of the need to find out if the clients were getting what they wanted, in order to adjust the work to better fit their stated needs. In one case, this meant being able to supply some written material to hand on to the next team of freelance deliverers.

> *I was there for a year and a half – I think my predecessor was there for a couple of years – we were calling in new directors; we were calling in new workshop leaders to run summer projects on a regular basis. So all the evaluations, whether it was from teachers or from participants in the summer schools or whatever particular project it might be, were very relevant when actually trying to kind of hand the remit to new artists and to new practitioners.*

In another, the clients' views were regarded as important because the education sector is changing so rapidly and evaluation was seen as a good way of keeping up with developments.

One director spoke of the need to identify the gaps between aims and realisation:

I think it's to capture, to read the patterns and processes of the development of the work, to explore the gap between aims and realisation and to offer back some analysis of where those gaps might be narrowed.

Another referred to finding out if one is achieving something valuable, even though it does not fall within the original aims. One interviewee regarded evaluation as one of the methods for ensuring that you don't get side-tracked; several companies talked of the range of demands on their resources, and the difficulty of rationalising refusals.

Securing funding

In the words of one Board member, '*it helps you prove that you are doing what you say you are doing, and then you get the cash*'. This blunt, but very realistic, analysis was echoed more gently elsewhere, but the intention to ensure the continuation of the work, to stop the work disappearing and to support the Black theatre sector were all quoted as reasons for evaluating. To satisfy the funders remained a potent reason to evaluate for many interviewees.

Reassurance

This reason had a number of supporters, which might suggest a level of insecurity amongst interviewees. One interviewee spoke of evaluation providing more motivation for the company: '*it's an improvement on "aren't we great?" hype*'. Others spoke of needing to maintain their confidence, and the value of positive feedback. A variation came in referring to the need to build more trust with the client group by involving them in the evaluation process.

3.12.2 Evaluation methods employed by the companies

Most companies seemed to use one or both of two methods of evaluation, these being written forms or questionnaires, or more informal, conversational means.

Written forms tended to be directed mainly at teachers, rather than at the pupils themselves, or at families in the case of one theatre that worked for school parties as well as family groups. One company had experimented with approaches to encourage young people to become more involved in evaluation.

We have just developed what we call chat-back cards, which is really evaluation sheets, but we are calling them chat-back cards and we get the actors to work with the young people to complete them without trying to influence them or influence what's said at all.

The same company was also investigating ways to use the internet to encourage feedback from young people. It favoured this above youth representation on its Board, which it felt would attract a very particular type of young person.

Informal, conversational methods included focus groups in one case, and another used one-to-one conversations with young people as a regular strategy. Only one company referred to debriefing meetings after each project.

Four of the ten companies mentioned external evaluation relating to recent projects. One of these was an Arts Council-funded evaluation at the end of the first part of a continuing process. Another had been working with a higher education institution in its region in an attempt to ascertain a more effective way of evaluating art practices and processes. A third was engaged in a study support project that was the subject of substantial evaluation by the DfEE, and the fourth mentioned ongoing evaluation by the drama adviser in the local education department.

One interviewee warned that one should be careful about what one feels, and not necessarily trust it, but others suggested that one just knows how something has gone, and that that was a significant part of evaluation.

3.12.3 The impact of evaluation

It was here that some gaps started to appear. One interviewee spoke of the lack of time to review the material gathered as part of the evaluation process. In another company, the intention to inform the next incoming freelance director was thwarted because little attempt was made to get the newcomer to read the material. Another spoke of not being aware of any meeting being held to discuss evaluation, despite everyone's commitment to it. One director was very direct in saying that evaluation had no influence on future work.

In addition, there were certain reservations about the usefulness of evaluation. One interviewee spoke of the difficulty of choosing what to take most note of, since in many cases very conflicting responses will be forthcoming. It appeared that the process of analysis had not been fully explored. Another identified a potential negative effect of evaluation.

> *I think evaluation is terribly useful, but in its place. I think there's a danger sometimes that evaluation can be the tail that wags the dog artistically, and I think evaluation is great, and I would hate to burden the young people with too much evaluation, because at the end of the day they are not here to do an academic course; they are here to have fun and really enjoy themselves and do theatre. So we are building in the evaluation, but in a way that we hope will be actually productive.*

This interviewee also resented the constant demand to justify the work, claiming that the sports lobby was not treated in the same manner.

The investment of resources in education work by the case study companies appeared to be very significant in every case. How their education activity related to the other aspects of the companies' work will be the subject of the next chapter.

4. THE RELATIONSHIP BETWEEN THE COMPANY'S EDUCATION PROGRAMME AND ITS OTHER ACTIVITIES

4.1 Overview

Whatever the primary purpose of each theatre company, each of them had to find ways to integrate the management of the artistic and educational aspects of their work. As far as the practice itself was concerned, some found it impossible to distinguish between the educational activities and the rest of the work, most had education activity either supporting, or supported by, other artistic activity, and some had education programmes running parallel to their core artistic programme.

There are a number of ways in which the educational elements of a company's programme integrate with its other activities. These may be organisational, artistic or audience related, and presuppose that integration is an appropriate approach to running an education programme, which need not necessarily be the case. It also presupposes that education is part of the theatre company's brief, and while all the case studies believed that it is, the reasons for this belief were various.

There was a widespread perception in the ten theatre companies that education had an appropriate status, and that this status was dependent partly on the overall purpose of each company. But it also depended on the commitment and status of key personnel in each organisation, especially the chief executive and education officer, or whoever led on education matters. The expectations of funders and the attitude of the Board could also be significant factors. However, there was a more critical view of the status accorded to education by some companies, and that was the view held by several freelance education deliverers. They generally felt that the status was not as high as it should have been. Their views may perhaps have differed from those of permanent company members because they had less investment, or less familiarity, with the companies for whom they worked. It may equally be that their perspective was more 'objective'.

Looking at the examples of education practice cited by the interviewees, a wide range of manifestations of integration was apparent, some demonstrating how education activity delivered the core aims of a company or how resources, be they staffing, financial, physical or artistic, were shared. Some interesting aspects of the relationship between education and artistic aims emerged, especially how the two can influence one another. However, there were aspects of integration that posed problems, and instances where a lack of integration resulted in negative effects.

Finally, there appeared to be a considerable amount of change taking place as far as education was concerned in the ten case studies. One may assume that this was in response to the extent of change in the various contexts in which they worked. The picture being drawn of education in theatre companies at the present time could well be substantially different in the fairly near future.

4.2   Meanings of integration

Having identified the ten case studies with variety in mind, it is hardly surprising that there was a limited degree of comparability amongst the theatres involved. In some respects, it is true in all the case studies that education was integrated with the core artistic activity. (For example, all had some artistic accountability through the company's artistic director, just as they had financial accountability through the administration.) However, that integration was different in each case, both in matters of degree and in the nature of the integration:

Having been in a situation where I've run an education department which has been absolutely at arm's length to a company, it's problematic. There is always a tension, but if the understanding that the contexts in which the elements of the organisation work are different – so the context of the education department is different from the context in which the work from the main stage works – but the mission is exactly the same.

We have classified the nature of the integration into three types, and in a few companies, more than one of these types are present.

4.2.1 Education projects which are the core artistic activity

This was perhaps the most difficult manifestation of integration to pin down, because it had at its heart the definition of what constitutes 'education' in the context of theatre. In this model, education ceased to be an activity with its own structures, methods and aims, and became instead a perspective or intention within all that was undertaken by a company. As such, it informed everything from the way the company was organised, to the selection of artistic material, to relations with bookers. Differentiating that position from that of a company that considered educational potential when scheduling its next season of plays was somewhat delicate. Although no repertory theatre cited a main house professional play as part of its education programme, several cited education activities related to such plays. A community touring company did cite a play that it was touring to small villages as part of its education programme. Without a full evaluation of projects, it would be impossible to ascertain whether one position was more 'educational' than the other.

The definition of what constituted an education project in these circumstances was difficult. A project may be consciously educational in its aims, and those aims may be explicit or implicit. Indeed, the playwright of one of the projects described identified his role thus:

> *I think that, perversely, my role is to disguise the educational content of the play.*

For the present, we have to reluctantly accept that we cannot formulate a definition of what constitutes an education project. The arguments and evidence put by case study companies asserting that all their work was educational was persuasive. However, an unsupported assertion that 'all theatre is educational' might be more difficult to accept.

4.2.2 Education programmes that either support, or are supported by, the core artistic programme

This is a widely supported approach to education work in regional repertory theatres, but is not confined to them. In many cases, companies have cited education activities designed to make more accessible or understandable the work on the main stage or the programme of touring productions, through Theatre Days, programme notes, post-show discussions, teachers' packs and education workshops. The overall intention seemed to be twofold: either to provide an educational experience that will make the theatre experience more meaningful (see aim B2, Chapter 2), or to use the stimulus of the theatre piece to contribute to the personal, educational or community development of the audience members (see aim D7, Chapter 2). In most cases, both of these intentions were present – audience development was both for the benefit of the theatre experience itself, and for the benefit of the individual members of the audience as learners.

Several interviewees regarded this symbiosis as central to the rationale for education work: the artistic product was the resource for education work, and the education work was what made the artistic product accessible to audiences.

4.2.3 Education programmes running parallel to the core artistic activity

This model is more akin to a holding company running two trading arms, but in the case studies there were always elements of closer integration than that would imply, and in none of the case studies were artistic cross-overs of some sort absent. Both the staffing and physical resources of the theatre itself were shared by the education operation. Although in all cases the planning of the artistic programme and the education programme met at some point in the organisational structure, the degree of integration could be minimal, relating more to the logistical allocation of human, physical and financial resources than to the creation of artistic coherence. Certainly, there were cases where an education project had taken place with apparently no relevance or connection with the main artistic programme, and this was not to suggest that the project was any less effective or valued for that. Indeed, it could be argued that the educational benefits could be enhanced if projects were not shackled to artistic programmes, and were able to be more pupil or client orientated.

4.3 Elements of integration

Whatever the overall nature of the integration of education with core artistic activity, we have identified a number of practical elements through which education relates to the rest of a theatre's activity.

4.3.1 Style of work

This was noted in one company, where the building dictated that all productions be in the round. This factor was deemed to be a particular strength of all of the education work as well.

4.3.2 Target audiences/clients

Several companies referred to the fact that their education work was aimed at the same sectors of the population as their main work. This applied particularly to companies having a distinct remit to work for particular people, such as the youth sector, cultural minorities of geographically disadvantaged communities. However, at least one company was deliberately using its education programme as a tool to widen involvement in its core artistic activity, indicating that it was consciously not working with its traditional clientele in its education projects.

4.3.3 Financial integration

Although some companies received limited proportions of their budgets for education work only, all integrated their education budgets with their overall budget. This seemed on the whole to be of benefit to education work, in some cases resulting in very large funds going to education projects. There was a clear return for many companies in that some believed that education was an important attraction for funders.

> *Any Lottery bid will founder if education is not reasonably central to its objectives.*

> *We're much more confident in our ability to fund our educational projects because the trusts and foundations, and increasingly the corporate sector, want the feel-good factor and an engagement with training and education. But we need to be able to fund the high-quality art, which has to be there to enable the education work.*

This has important implications. Many interviewees were at pains to claim that they did not do education projects simply because the funding was being offered for it – they had to know that the work fitted in with their aims and did not compromise their work:

I don't know whether this is spin or whether it's true or how much it is reflected across other organisations, but we've never ever chased money and there are people queuing up at the moment and asking to give us money to do different things, many of which are very specifically, tightly focused on educational aims. That isn't the reason why we do them; the reason we do them is can we do them, can we do the work well?

But at the same time the pressure to create income in order to survive could be intense. While education often benefited from the overall financial pot, there may well be some pressure to also contribute to it when possible. It can require considerable integrity and rigour to handle the pressure to accept money, as was apparent in the example quoted in Chapter 3 (3.2.2).

One company was on paper making a profit on its education workshop programme, and thus subsidising its core budget. However, the hidden subsidy of core staff time would have far outweighed that gain. This would also be true of any other company: where education budgets appeared to be quite limited, the hidden subsidy in terms of staffing, use of premises and administrative and management could be very significant.

4.3.4 Shared staffing

This aspect of integration was seen as very important, especially by education staff.

They get to work so closely with the professional technicians of the theatre, ... an apprenticeship model.

Although the contribution of artistic staff was also valued, it was the technical personnel, in lighting, construction, etc. who often formed the bridge between the two parts, since artistic staff were so often temporary freelance workers. Although some theatres had dedicated education administrators, in others administrative support was shared with the rest of the organisation. However, several interviewees stressed the importance of high artistic expertise as a crucial resource in delivering education projects.

I think the distinctive thing is that the Artistic Director is the one who is running it and that our Artistic Director has an international reputation ... I mean the quality of what [our director] *is delivering is high because ... well we can tell that because they* [teachers] *tell us!*

4.3.5 Use of core artistic product

It was widely, but not universally, felt that education work should relate to the core artistic activity; '*otherwise what's the point of education work*'.

It was felt by several interviewees that the core artistic activity was the true resource for the education activities, giving them their distinctiveness and appeal to educators and learners. This usually manifested itself in the form of education projects being attached to productions, often using the expertise of the artists involved in the production, sometimes mediated through an education specialist.

4.3.6 Core artistic product as a source for education projects

One company cited education projects that had emerged from previous artistic activities, which had inspired a desire to exploit the talents of the artists involved and make them available as a learning resource to others. The case of a French pyrotechnician being introduced to disaffected youths showed particular flair.

4.4 Is integration desirable?

There appeared to be a considerable majority in favour of the view that integration of the education programme with the core artistic activity was appropriate. This view was very strongly held by some.

> *If you're going to have an education remit, then it is absolutely ridiculous not to use what's happening in the main theatre. It's ridiculous not to work with them ... it's all there to be used ... if they don't work together, it would be a waste ... a terrible waste of opportunities if they didn't.*

But others were more cautious in their support for the view.

> *If the purpose of the education work is to access the artistic work, you need to be careful the education work does not become subservient, unless that is its specific purpose.*

Another interviewee expressed concern lest education should become the tail that wags the dog. This would appear to be a very unlikely scenario, given the apparently minor influence that education had in the selection of the main artistic programme in most companies (see below), though one interviewee felt that education could sometimes take up too much attention:

> *From an Administrative Producer point of view, I think we can often dedicate far more time to evolving our education programme – almost more than we do sometimes to our commissioned work.*

This balance was crucial for many interviewees, who variously expressed the view that the artistic activity was the education resource, and unless that was kept central the validity of the education programme was cast into doubt.

There was also a view that not all of the education work needed to be related to the core artistic programme, and that not all of the main programme needed to have education attached to it.

No I don't think we should have education work around everything that we do.

Why? I think you flatten the landscape out ... I think there should be mountains and trees ...

Another warned that integration should not be 'gratuitous' and should only be undertaken when educationally valid.

This research project had no remit to ascertain either the artistic or the educational effectiveness of projects offered by the case study theatres. Therefore, whether integration of education with core artistic activity resulted in either better art or better education was not explored. Further research may be appropriate on this issue.

4.5 Is education perceived as part of the theatre's brief?

No company regarded education as being beyond their remit, but each saw different reasons for its inclusion.

For several companies, education was a requirement of funding, although except in the case of specific project grants, this did not apply to arts funding sources. Local authority funding was more frequently specifically allocated for the delivery of an education service, and even where that was not explicit, the company may regard the delivery of an education programme as an expectation, if not a requirement. In one case, the company believed that the education work was the tacit justification for the core funding of the theatre.

There was very widespread support for the view that education work was an important aspect of audience development, but this was not seen primarily as a way of increasing audiences for the core artistic programme. There was a much more general commitment to giving people that chance to experience the arts at first hand, a commitment to a form of cultural inclusion. For one theatre, this presented a problem in that they perceived themselves to be the only major cultural resource in their area, and found it difficult to say no to requests for work. Another company handled this problem by establishing two complete units to undertake the delivery and coordination of participatory activities in their region.

4.6 Factors influencing the status of education in theatre companies

Almost all interviewees felt that the status of education in their company was fairly or very high. Those least likely to take that view were freelance education specialists who worked for short periods with one, and in some cases, several companies. Their criticisms included:

I don't think the programme is thought about in terms of young people. I think that the standard of the work and the standard of the performers who take part in the work needs to be recognised. And I think that giving it more status would also raise all those standards.

In a way the term 'education' gets in the way. We should be talking about what the theatre provides broadly, to all audiences. Education is seen to be for young people – it should be open to all.

Certain factors would seem to affect the status of education, although it may possibly be the case that the strength of the education work itself has an impact on the way the company is organised as well.

4.6.1 The commitment of the chief executive (or artistic director)

Although they tended not to claim the credit themselves, it would appear that the chief executive had a very great influence on the status of education. This was often most clearly seen in the smaller companies, where the chief executive was more closely involved in all aspects of the work, although even in the largest company studied, the chief executive had a significant direct involvement in the education activities. In another company, the newly arrived artistic director was clearly indicating an intention to radically overhaul the profile of the education work.

It would appear that their professional background was significant in generating their commitment. In some cases, this may be a generation issue, with several people now in top positions who had started out when education was a growth area in theatre in the 1970s and 80s. Several had worked in theatre in education companies, been in charge of education programmes, or previously run education activities. All had some previous experience in education work in some form. Some also cited family relationships as informing their attitude to education work.

4.6.2 The place of the education officer

Some companies have no identified education officer. In one company, the post had been lost because of financial constraints, and the absence was seen by some as a weakness, and certainly put additional pressure on the rest of the organisation. Two companies had no education officer out of choice, the role being carried out by the chief executive or artistic director. In both cases, it was widely agreed that this raised the status of the work. In the words of a freelance assistant director involved in education delivery:

I think, ... the strength as it stands is that there is an awful lot of involvement at ... I mean it's not a huge company but everyone is involved in the process and I think the dangers are if you had an Education Officer that possibly you would have to be sure not to lose that, as I think it's very important.

In another company, the imperative to get the company's artistic core established meant that no education post had yet been established, and the consensus was that as a result the education work was not as developed as it should be. One company, running with a temporary education officer, and going through some radical development following the arrival of a new artistic director, was expressing general dissatisfaction with the state of its education work.

Three companies could be said to have well-established education directors. In the case of the largest company in the research, the postholder was not part of the highest level of senior management, and may not be directly involved in all stages of planning. In another, the education director was a very influential member of the senior management team, was closely involved in all artistic planning, and since taking up the post was agreed to have been very influential in the overall direction of the company. A third education director was also on the senior management team, and was always consulted at an early stage in the overall planning process.

Whether or not through an education post, it seemed significant that whoever was the driving force concerning education should be part of the senior management team, or have a dedicated champion there.

4.6.3 External pressures/encouragement

Some companies were very explicitly encouraged to develop their education activities for outside sources: one through the demands of potential clients (which posed some prioritisation problems) and another through encouragement from the main funder to set up new participatory arts wings. In the latter case, the company seemed not to be concerned that its remit was being stretched, regarding it as an extension and compliment to its already existing commitment to the needs of its catchment area. One company felt that the expectations of the local authority funder were for a significant education service, and this seems to have contributed to the scale, if not the status, of the education work.

4.6.4 The attitude of the Board

This presented a rather curious picture, in that the support expressed by the Board members interviewed was not matched by their knowledge of the company's education activities.

You asked me if I'd seen educational activity and I told you that I hadn't ... it isn't part of those things which I do, but it probably should be, or most certainly should be, but I have to say that I haven't actually been a witness to education activity in the field ... though I don't see the work, I have a lively interest in what is going on, and therefore I feel very satisfied, I'm glad of the satisfaction, from this organisation having what I know is a vigorous and productive educational programme.

Another Board member recognised the importance of its education programme to the overall purpose of the company.

I mean the board was very, very enthusiastic and that project was developed because it was thought to be actually very significant and socially significant that a company like this addressed that and that clearly has a huge number of education possibilities.

Although experienced in supporting education in his previous work, he expressed some reticence in attending education activities.

I mean if I said to [the director] *'Do you mind if I come along?', I think he would say 'Fine, great', you know. I'm not sure how I would feel that ... you know, 'Why is* [name] *coming out?'. You know what I mean?*

It may well be the less public nature of most education work that inhibited Board members from monitoring or supporting education work more actively. But there is no doubt from the statements of interviewees that Boards enthusiastically supported the work in theory, and indeed expressed pride in the fact that their company was engaged in that way.

Another Board member, because of his background in education, and perhaps because of the management ethos of the company, had become much more directly involved in the education work, and was more familiar with it. Another had even worked directly on study support material for an education project.

4.6.5 The purpose of the company

It almost goes without saying that the status of education is likely to be higher in a company whose main purpose is educational – '*The whole aim is educational – the word may not be there, but the meaning is*'. But this rather begs the question, how did the central purpose come to be education in the first place? One such company embraced education having been previously only an international festival. Another had evolved to its present form from having been a political theatre company. A third was initially a community theatre company. In each case, the emergence of a commitment to education seems to have been evolutionary, and in response to prevailing circumstances, opportunity and the interest of company members. To compare the relative status of education between companies would be inappropriate. Even where education is not the primary purpose of the company, the commitment to it can be very powerful and strongly supported.

4.7 What does integration mean in practice?

The following examples illustrate ways in which education is integrated into the wider artistic programme of organisations. (For this section, we have avoided examples from companies who claimed that education was the main purpose.)

♦ A company specialising in presenting new and contemporary writing selected its artistic material for its artistic quality, but also because it was very challenging. The education workshops contributed to making the work accessible to audiences, as did the style of performance itself. The aims were integrated, and the artistic product was the resource for the education work.

♦ A small building-based company presented all of its productions in the round. The education workshops that prepared students for an experience of theatre in the round focused in part on that aspect of theatre.

♦ A regional repertory theatre invested the time and expertise of all of its technical staff in mounting a community production, ensuring that the human, financial and physical resources of the organisation were put to educational use for a large number of participants. They then experienced making theatre in much the same way as professional theatre artists do.

♦ A company specialising in the commissioning and presentation of new writing by and for Black people mounted a major festival event, which included a series of debates, led by experienced professionals, to explore the issues relating to culture and the Black experience. The educational component was integrated into the time and space of the overall event.

4.8 How do education aims relate to overall artistic aims?

Some interviewees were disinclined to make any distinction between the two spheres of aims: '*I just don't ever perceive these two separate things.*'

4.8.1 Their influence on each other

Although in some cases rather puzzled by the distinction, and even perhaps slightly affronted by the enquiry, interviewees had some revealing comments on the relationship. These suggested a kind of symbiosis between educational and artistic aims.

> *I think it* [education] *feeds the whole vision hugely, hugely. You know there is no question that it is so central to what we do that none of us would even imagine not pursuing it with a vigour and commitment that we do.*

This came from an artistic director of an organisation that had not started out with an education priority, but had ended up with a full-blown commitment to education, to the point where it was arguably equally significant as the rest of the artistic programme. That view, of education feeding the artistic view, was complemented by the view of the same company's education officer: '*I think certainly the educational aims are very much driven from those core aims.*'

The two views suggested a distinctive, but entirely complementary, relationship between the two aims, and it is worth noting that the company's concern to protect and develop the purely 'artistic' elements of the operation was essential if valid educational projects were to exist as well. A third view, from the marketing director in the same company, really centralised education in relation to the core aims: '*The education work is the only aspect which really fulfils that* [main artistic] *aim.*'

4.8.2 Their separation from each other

All this is in stark contrast to a view from the other end of the spectrum.

Generally speaking they operate quite discretely.

In pointing this out, we must make quite clear that we have no reason to suppose that the resulting outcomes were any less valuable or valued as a result. However, given the number of comments referring to the core artistic activity as the real resource for education work, it may be that too discrete an operation means less exploitation of potential that could be achieved.

Such a separation can also lead to frustration, and can lead to a one-way road of respect and appreciation.

> *... there was not a lot of integration between the basic programme, the core programme of the community department and the core programme on stage at all times. However, because the children and young people in the area were coming on a regular basis to see plays at* [the theatre] *and because they were having [the theatre's] actors in their school, they were actually very familiar with the theatre. Most primary school children that I met and talked to, and I went to many, many schools while I was there, said 'Oh yeah, we've been to the theatre and we've seen this, this and this' ... so they had a relationship with the theatre – so in terms of future audiences, in terms of outreaching, in terms of the theatre being a community ...*

The same interviewee saw another side of the relationship as well.

> *... when I see, for example, the core acting company didn't come and see the children's shows, or when I felt that everyone was just wishing that the 300 noisy children would just get out because it was really noisy and they left sweet papers and we had to clear it up, those were the things that I found frustrating ... and when I*

saw actors who I thought were wonderful in the education company who weren't being seen for main house plays because they were education actors ...

The education work may well have been delivering an audience development aim, and may well have been delivering excellent education projects, but integration was apparently not the cause. In the words of a Board member:

I don't think this organisation could survive credibly if it wasn't doing that work; therefore, I regard it as being extremely important.

4.8.3 The changing relationship between education and core aims

In another theatre, where the recently appointed education officer expressed great admiration for the management and the support they gave him, the attitude was not yet what might be hoped for:

Still, at the end of the day, people think principally what we are here to do is put on six shows in that main house, and everything else we do is additional.

This was one of a number of theatres in the sample in which education had been given additional attention in the very recent past, where integration had become part of the intention. Such a sea change cannot be realised instantly, but half our case studies were engaged in a radical shift in their approach to education, and one might assume that the overall picture could look very different in a year or so.

4.8.4 Education aims separate *and* central

For one chief executive, the education work was a key component in delivering a very large brief, and although he believed that the cross-over of staff between the main and the education work was highly beneficial, the two aspects remained largely separate.

We are here to provide a quality and a very broad range of service ... you know, it is a kind of cultural flagship in this part of the world and if we don't do it then it doesn't get done at a certain level and scale here and we fill that obligation very seriously, I think. Now in terms of there being an obvious symbiosis between the nature of our artistic policy and the nature of our education policy as I said before ... no, actually they kind of run in parallel somehow and they rely on each other.

One of his senior management team, having defined the overall mission partly in financial terms, put education as very much part of the overall creative mission.

I think they [education policies] complement it. I think the whole ethos behind that policy is that education should be at the centre of what we do. We should be revolving around those educational aspirations, which is why I don't believe that the educational ... heart of this building is just the education department.

4.8.5 Education aims as deliberately separate

For one interviewee, admittedly in a theatre where there was a consensus of dissatisfaction with their recent track record on education, and a collective commitment to address it, a quite different view was taken.

I think that people who work in arts education do want their autonomy – they do not necessarily see themselves as simply the illuminator, or explainer, of the main stage; they see themselves as generating original work ... education departments and people who run education departments have the mindset of producers, rather than teachers – they see themselves as producing educational theatre rather than teaching, not as servants of the main activity.

The view has considerable validity. Many people working in a creative industry and constantly exposed to creative activity want to be creative themselves, and creativity is served by some autonomy from structures, rules and policies. But creativity takes place in specific contexts, and balancing autonomy against making the best use of resources and opportunities, while fulfilling needs, is a great challenge, both for artists and for those who seek to 'manage' them.

4.9   Clarity and consensus of vision

From the large volume of interviews undertaken for this research, two distinct results emerged. First, within each company there appeared to be a general consensus concerning the quality and success (or otherwise in one case) of their education work. Within most companies, a shared level of enthusiasm and commitment to the education work was revealed. A sense of pride, excitement and almost crusading spirit was often evident. In many companies, this was shared by those only laterally connected to the education work. There was a case where an individual admitted that the work did not really interest him, but even there the support for the existence of the work was very genuine. In the one company where there was dissatisfaction with the education work, it was shared by all the interviewees, and seemed to have resulted in a unanimous commitment to correct it.

However, there were discernibly different attitudes between people fulfilling different functions. Board members, while being very supportive of the education work, were frequently uninformed about what was happening, and their perspective was often dominated by the financial implications of the education activity, both as income generation and as expenditure.

Chief executives, understandably, presented a very clear and supportive view of the activities of their staff. All bar one were confident that the status and level of integration between education and core work were as they should be, even though they were a little different in each company. In the exceptional case, the chief executive's view was shared by the rest of the staff.

Education officers were predictably enthusiastic about their patch, and were very fulsome about the support they received from their management. In the words of one education director:

> There's never been a moment, I think ... we've had our difficult moments at difficult times ... but there's never been a moment when I felt that actually the two chief executives here have ever, ever wavered from the decision that they made to invest in me.

Another broadened that sense of support:

> I needed a lot of support from the rest of the building and I got that support and actually, you know, that helped me grow and helped me develop and because we had that support. Finally the education department was able to do things that it hadn't been able to do before.

As indicated earlier, the most critical group of theatre workers were the freelance mediators of education projects, or those who were past members of the company. Perhaps because they were less inhibited, less needful of balancing education against other priorities in an organisation, or merely fighting their corner more, they tended to be the ones who felt most strongly that education was not getting the support or resources it deserved. Because they are so often mediators without the capacity to influence policy decisions, perhaps they were more likely to focus on shortcomings, and it may be appropriate for companies to find receptive systems for taking their perspectives into account.

4.10 The state of change for education in theatre companies

Given the rapidity of change in our cultural and educational worlds at the present time, it would be most disturbing if this was not reflected in theatre companies involved in educational activities. On analysis, the extent of change, and the fundamental nature of some of the changes, were quite startling.

♦ One company saw its education work at the time as '*an aspiration*' and regarded itself as on the verge of translating this into a reality (though the amount of their work that would be classified as education by many companies was already substantial).

♦ A company that unanimously regarded its education work as unsatisfactory looked set to alter its approach considerably with the arrival of a new artistic director.

- A large building-based company was about to take possession of new premises that will be used substantially for education activities, thus transforming their education programme as a whole.

- One organisation had plans well under way to develop a new strand of work around research and evaluation: '*Something that we've never done, we've focused on intermittently but it's about the evidence, not just the evidence of process but the evidence about public interactions and about where it fits aesthetically, culturally, socially within this city, and in five years' time come up with some findings which we hope will be profoundly influential to a number of people.*'

- A company that had until recently been essentially a community touring theatre company had extended its remit to include all aspects of participatory arts in its geographical area: '*Clearly, the reason that the participatory arts programme was bid for by the company was because it felt that presenting plays to an audience was only part of the story. But it's not an add-on to do this. If you like, it's an extension of the aims of what we wanted to do. It's to animate those audiences.*'

Perhaps because education is not a clearly defined mandatory activity, with specific funding attached to it, except in the case of rather peripheral or short-term grants, education can be subject to considerable changes of fortune. When enthused or visionary people take up key positions, they can have a dramatic impact on the extent and clarity of the education work undertaken. In one company, a recently appointed education director had already earned the respect of senior management and was very influential on the senior management team. Another was credited as having a central influence in putting education at the very front end of a company's thinking and practice. Many interviewees agreed that where such inspiration and commitment to education were absent, then perhaps an education programme ought to be absent too. But one education specialist said:

I would fight professionally and personally to have that [commitment to education] in every arts organisation in this country.

5.   SUMMARY AND CONCLUSION

5.1   The study

With the overall aim of encouraging good practice through the clarification of the aims and activities of theatre company education work, the research reported here addressed four key objectives:

♦   to analyse the aims and purposes of education work in theatre companies;

♦   to examine how these aims are translated into practice;

♦   to investigate the relationship between the educational work and the overall artistic mission of the theatre companies and how the identity of a theatre company relates to their education policy; and

♦   to use the results of the research to inform developments in the policy and practice of theatre company education activity and to develop the policy of funding bodies to better suit the needs of companies and artists.

The research was undertaken through interviews with staff from ten theatre companies, selected to ensure a range of sizes, style and location. It in no way aimed to evaluate, assess or appraise the education activities of theatre companies. Rather, it sought to examine the range of education work being provided, and its aims and intentions.

5.2   Theatre companies' educational aims

The pattern of perceived aims which surfaced from the interviews was complex, and, as acknowledged by several interviewees, diverse intentions were frequently interrelated.

Analysis of company members' responses produced five broad categories of aims, each with its own set of sub-categories. The five main categories were identified in Chapter 2 as follows:

♦   educational aims totally integrated with artistic aims;

♦   drama/theatre-centred educational aims;

♦   curriculum development and support;

♦   client-centred educational aims; and

♦   aims relating to the needs of theatre companies.

'Client-centred' aims (i.e. those relating to the personal development of individual participants and/or community development) emerged undeniably as an overriding preoccupation, with notably more citations than either curriculum-centred aims, or those concerned with theatre companies' artistic or financial survival. Three companies claimed that educational aims were totally integrated with core artistic aims.

The unmistakable conviction of company members' views on the unique contribution of theatre to education afforded striking resonance with a 'client-centred' approach. Three distinct but interrelated interpretations of the role of theatre in education were discernible in the data:

♦ a means of communication through emotion and/or the imagination to challenge preconceptions, and to extend and enhance understanding of ourselves and others;

♦ a source of opportunities for self-expression which empowers individuals and generates self-esteem by allowing them to take risks, and release potential creativity; and

♦ a collective/community artform.

The majority of companies acknowledged changes in their educational aims over recent years, and reported an increase in educational activity. This could be for a variety of reasons. In some cases, companies had undertaken a radical reappraisal of their overall mission. In others, the development of opportunities for collaboration, with schools or through partnerships with other organisations, had accelerated their educational activities.

The role of the chief executive was held to be a crucial component of a coherent and committed approach to education. The interest of the Board appeared to vary considerably from one company to another, but where members of the Board had an interest or experience in education, their contribution was valued. Some interviewees reported the significance of a company's size on the communication of educational aims to respective members; communication was generally believed to be less effective in larger companies with separate education departments.

In addition to long-term funding, many interviewees contended that greater flexibility in funding arrangements would enable them to be more creative, and more effective, in achieving their educational goals. Funding from various sources had enabled all ten companies to develop their education work. However, many senior managers argued that increased flexibility would considerably enhance their ability to generate a continuing and progressive education programme.

5.3 Translating aims into practice

Having analysed and explored the aims of the case study companies, Chapter 3 investigated the practice that emerges from those aims. Working from one project example from each company, it was possible to identify some recurrent features both in the generation and nature of education projects. However, the extent of differences between projects was marked, reflecting the variety of identities and contexts of the companies involved.

There was a clear overall pattern of projects being originated and managed by core company staff, while being delivered or mediated by freelance staff in the vast majority of cases. Many projects were the result of partnerships between arts organisations. The reliance on freelance staff, and the various implications of this state of affairs, have been a recurrent feature of the research.

The projects that were described divided fairly evenly between two broad types:

♦ those that supported, or were supported by, core artistic product, and

♦ participatory activities, using the theatre expertise available to the company, designed with particular sectors of the community in mind.

In some cases, a valid claim was made that the education project described was part of the core activity of the company.

The education projects described were targeted at a wide range of participants, including the fullest age range, and those within and outside of the formal education sector, including various community groupings. It became very clear from project descriptions that audience development and the delivery of education aims were frequently outcomes deriving from the same activity.

Analysis of the project case studies suggested a high degree of consistency between the rhetoric or stated aims of theatre companies' education programmes and the reality of what was mounted in practice. Projects that might deliver aims relating to curriculum development and teacher support were much less prevalent than those with 'client-centred' aims.

Evaluation was approached enthusiastically by some, and cautiously by others. This in part reflected resource limitations, but in some cases revealed a scepticism about the impact of an investment in evaluation.

5.4 Education programmes and core artistic activity

Apart from financial, managerial and administrative integration, education work appeared to be integrated with the rest of a theatre's work in three different ways. For some companies, **education was the core activity**; for some, **education projects supported, or were supported by, the core artistic activity**; and for others, **education projects ran parallel to the core artistic activity**, and were not integrated. Several companies combined more than one of these forms of integration. There was a general belief that resources were best used through integration, but this was qualified by the fear that one side – usually the core artistic imperative – might overwhelm the other.

It was the generally held view that corporate or collective support for education, from the Board and chief executive down, determined the well-being of education programmes. Where there was criticism of theatre companies for their attitude to education, it tended to be expressed more by the freelance theatre workers who were interviewed. It may be appropriate for companies to find receptive systems for taking their perceptions into account.

It was widely agreed that the education work undertaken by companies was dependent on the maintenance of quality in the core artistic work they undertook. The core artistic activity and expertise in a theatre were a fundamental resource for the education work. In its turn, the education work was generally seen to contribute to the well-being of the parent theatre company. Recognising, exploiting and enhancing this symbiosis were of benefit to the theatre companies, their education programmes, and the beneficiaries of education programmes in the wider world. However, symbiosis is different from integration.

The view was expressed by some interviewees that the integration of core artistic activity and education work might bring some negative results. Not all education work needed to relate to the main artistic programme, not all theatre workers were equipped to deliver education work, and the focus on an education perspective could even result in taking the eye off the larger artistic ball. Many interviewees argued that while it would be desirable for all theatres to involve themselves closely in educational activities, they should only do so if both committed and equipped to do so. While some interviewees asserted that teachers value the exposure to the professional expertise of the theatre as a whole, their educational needs may not be best met by slavishly following an agenda created primarily for a theatre's convenience. According to the data, it is clearly essential that the educational needs of clients are appropriately addressed when using the resources of the theatre company, and that an integration of programming is not pursued simply as a matter of convenience or financial expediency.

5.5 Overarching issues and themes

Although Chapters 1 to 4 focused on different aspects of theatre and their education programmes, certain recurrent issues emerged and were illuminated throughout the research process.

5.5.1 Defining education projects

Companies classified a very wide range of projects as 'educational', in particular blurring the distinction between education and community development. With funding increases for education work by theatres due in the next few years, the question demands further consideration. Their approach to both policy and practice would suggest that companies did not see their role as restricted to the delivery or support of curriculum objectives. But they did regard the impact of theatre on individuals and communities as potentially educational. The question then arises as to what extent the aims and intentions of theatre work should be transparent and explicit, or even apparent. The variety of interpretations of 'educational' would seem to suggest that any attempt to circumscribe the definition might risk excluding valuable work, or alternatively being so broad and bland as to be meaningless. However, claims for educational validity need to be substantiated in some way, and criteria for establishing the educational credentials of any theatre work might need to be considered.

5.5.2 The role of theatres in the formal education context

Of the ten theatres studied as part of this research, seven regularly worked in schools, two others having a more limited or very recent involvement, and one having no school remit. Of the seven that did such work regularly, the proportion of their education programmes that were school related varied from a very large majority to a quite small minority. Overall, the relationship with schools merits some separate attention.

If theatres are not primarily charged with supporting or delivering the curriculum, either in schools, the youth sector or in community education, what service do they provide for those who are being educated or who are responsible for education? And how do they enter into dialogue with those who give them access to learners, in whatever context? Most of the work described in this report would appear to be the result of proactive initiatives on the part of the theatre companies, exercising their own artistic judgement and assessing the educational needs that they believe they can usefully address. This was often informed by dialogue with educators, and some companies maintained regular forums or channels of communication. However, even where such forums did exist or have existed, several companies indicated that there were difficulties in sustaining a productive dialogue.

Some interviewees even expressed scepticism about the potential of working in schools, and that the relationship with teachers and the curriculum was not entirely satisfactory. There was also recognition of the pressures teachers were under, and a perception that they experienced a lack of manoeuvrability in accommodating or exploiting the contribution of theatre companies, and a lack of time to plan with companies. It would appear that some companies had been more proactive than others in pursuing dialogues with teachers, but they, no doubt, were also subjected to time pressure.

It may well be appropriate to encourage opportunities or channels for improving understanding and communication between the two sides, possibly regenerating what many believe to have been a stronger relationship between theatre companies and teachers, as individuals or collectively, in the past. Finding more time to do this, for example by creating school liaison posts, or refining the language through which each side can better understand, and therefore contribute to, the relationship, may both be necessary.

In describing their educational aims, interviewees generally did not come up with succinct 'sound bites', and the educational output of theatre companies was not readily classifiable, either as individual companies or collectively. This can be regarded as a great strength, offering surprising and diverse alternative approaches and interventions in what are often regarded by teachers as difficult areas of exploration. It may also be an impediment to advocacy, especially to education policy makers who may be too preoccupied with other imperatives to have time to fully explore the potential role of theatre companies in schools. Stating the case for investment in the educational work of theatre companies would be much easier if it centred on the delivery of particular skills, but companies are striving to fulfil much wider needs, and believe that the contribution that theatre can make to education is both complex and fundamental. In the words of one artistic director:

> *Theatre is about communication, it's about ideas, it's about enthusiasm, and it's that whole thing about having a creative capital within our society, thinking human beings, not the kind of factory fodder that the Victorians needed, for example. Now you need a thinking, intelligent, innovative population, and theatre ... is in a really strong position to do that and to deliver that.*

Others referred to the collective aspect of the work, the rigour of generating product to deadline, the liveness of the experience, emotional as well as an intellectual understanding, and self confidence. That is only a sample of the types of claims made for theatre as a contributor to education, and this more complex approach may be harder to portray. Refining the language of definition, analysis and advocacy, without forfeiting any of the richness and variety of the activity, will be very challenging.

5.5.3 Variety and consensus

Theatre companies have grown from different roots, in different contexts, and their education work reflects those variations. While there would be no benefit in attempting to homogenise this picture, learning from each other's differences, as well as sharing similarities, could promote greater development in the future. Few would disagree that companies need to be aware of the range of aims and methods of work that may be available to them, so that they can debate and re-form these as appropriate. Evidence suggests that the mechanisms for enabling this to happen are either absent or not sufficiently accessible to all practitioners. Certainly, this is not being achieved through any training opportunities, since very few interviewees indeed have received training for their work in education, and there were very few common references to networking opportunities. It may be useful to encourage more forums for debate and work sharing. Perhaps the typology of aims offered in this report could sharpen the focus in considering the aims of theatre education programmes.

5.5.4 Continuity, development and progression

A number of factors have considerable influence on the potential for companies to develop their work and offer a clearer progression of opportunities to their clients. The high level of enthusiasm, sophistication and commitment in the companies studied could well produce even greater returns if certain factors were addressed.

There is a perception that the balance of funding has shifted from medium- or long-term funding (generating stability and the capacity to plan and develop), to short-term funding initiatives, many of which are seen as prescriptive and inhibiting of creativity and development. The perceived need to shoehorn creative ideas into restrictive funding requirements was seen as time consuming and limiting.

For most companies, education projects cannot be funded out of core revenue. When there is a dependence on project funding, rather than core funding, it is almost impossible to maintain permanent or long-term staff to deliver or mediate education work. This necessitates constantly retraining and reorientating the mediators, eating up expensive freelance and permanent staff time. There were a few cases where frequently used individual freelance workers were able to contribute to a developmental approach to the work, but this seemed to be the exception.

This prevalent reliance on freelance workers to mediate education projects brings other problems. The mediators are the people who come face to face with the teachers and students on a regular basis, but if they are constantly changing, this may inhibit the accumulation of a meaningful, trusting relationship that could result in a real development of the work itself. The mediators then become mere 'deliverers'. Although some companies were able to consolidate relationships with teachers in such circumstances, it was certainly not the case all round.

Concern was expressed that the pool of available freelance theatre education workers needed to meet the demand for the work is depleting. Because of their freelance status, it is difficult for freelance workers to have financial access to those training opportunities that do exist, and on-the-job training can be time consuming. Some were concerned that the financial insecurity of freelance work might mean ceasing to work in this field. The culture of transience may discourages individuals from committing themselves to such work in the first place, or from taking up such initial training opportunities as do exist.

But their temporary status, as it exists at present, does have certain advantages. Freelance arts workers might be regarded as modern equivalents of the roving mediaeval peddlers, carrying news of new techniques and perspectives from company to company. Certainly their specialist expertise was highly valued by many interviewees, and companies seemed to benefit greatly from their experience. Their outsider status in company establishments appeared to generate a tendency to be more critical of the work and the way it is handled by companies, but it is not clear to what extent companies were able to learn from their critical assessments. For their part, some freelance workers clearly preferred the freedom of their status, while companies retained the flexibility to engage artists to suit the particular needs of each project.

Balancing these different factors may be difficult, and it may be that the following strategies would address some of these issues:

♦   a more accessible provision of training opportunities;

♦   improved communication and dialogue between companies;

♦   some increase in the capacity to employ more education project mediators long term; and

♦   a more proactive approach to gathering the views of freelance workers.

This would necessitate an examination of funding practices and priorities, and in particular a reconsideration of the role and contribution of the freelance workers currently engaged. The points made above might lead one to suppose that more long-term employment would be advantageous to companies, to the development of the work and to the freelance workers themselves.

5.6 Conclusion

The ten theatre companies studied as part of this research presented a wide variation of characteristics in terms of size, remit, geographical features and purpose. They have consequently developed a similarly wide range of educational aims and of models for delivering those aims. The resulting impression may seem disparate and unfocused, and certainly defies any attempt at simple definition or classification. This diversity seems to be a strength, but may come at a price. Because the identity of the overall field is so complex, it may be difficult to promote the work, especially to policy makers who may have little direct contact with the work itself, and this applies to theatre Board members, as well as other arts and education policy makers. It would be unwise to attempt to impose a conformity upon companies concerning their education work, but ensuring greater dialogue and understanding could prove valuable, so that the field as a whole can develop to embrace the opportunities that are rapidly approaching.